THE

VOICE OF THE NEGRO 1919

Robert T. Kerlin

ARNO PRESS and THE NEW YORK TIMES
NEW YORK 1968

General Editor
WILLIAM LOREN KATZ

THE FOLLOWING WORK IS A COMPILATION FROM THE colored press of America for the four months immediately succeeding the Washington riot. It is designed to show the Negro's reaction to that and like events following, and to the World War and the discussion of the Treaty. It may, in the editor's estimation, be regarded as a primary document in promoting a knowledge of the Negro, his point of view, his way of thinking upon race relations, his grievances, his aspirations, his demands. Virtually the entire Afro-American press, consisting of two dailies, a dozen magazines, and nearly three hundred weeklies, has been drawn upon. Here is the voice of the Negro, and his heart and mind. Here the Negro race speaks as it thinks on the question of questions for America—the race question. The like of this utterance, in angry protest and prayerful pleading, the entire rest of the world does not offer.

When I told a publisher that I was making this compilation he remarked that my book would make disagreeable reading. There are worse things than disagreeable reading.

Robert T. Kerlin
JANUARY 1, 1920

THE VOICE OF THE NEGRO

Conference group of Negro editors, with a few white friends, in Washington, during the war.

THE VOICE OF
THE NEGRO
1919

BY

ROBERT T. KERLIN
PROFESSOR OF ENGLISH, VIRGINIA MILITARY INSTITUTE

NEW YORK
E. P. DUTTON & COMPANY
681 FIFTH AVENUE

Printed in the United States of America

PREFACE

The following work is a compilation from the colored press of America for the four months immediately succeeding the Washington riot. It is designed to show the Negro's reaction to that and like events following, and to the World War and the discussion of the Treaty. It may, in the editor's estimation, be regarded as a primary document in promoting a knowledge of the Negro, his point of view, his way of thinking upon race relations, his grievances, his aspirations, his demands. Virtually the entire Afro-American press, consisting of two dailies, a dozen magazines, and nearly three hundred weeklies, has been drawn upon. Here is the voice of the Negro, and his heart and mind. Here the Negro race speaks as it thinks on the question of questions for America—the race question. The like of this utterance, in angry protest and prayerful pleading, the entire rest of the world does not offer.

When I told a publisher that I was making this compilation he remarked that my book would make disagreeable reading. There are worse things than disagreeable reading.

THE EDITOR.

Lexington, Va., January 1, 1920.

▼

ACKNOWLEDGMENTS

To the Associated Negro Press and to the various magazines that I have quoted I wish to make grateful acknowledgment of their kindness in freely permitting me to use their copyright matter. To scores of weeklies beyond those for which I subscribed I am indebted for numerous free copies kindly supplied me on my application.

TABLE OF CONTENTS

INTRODUCTION

vii

Table of Contents

INTRODUCTION

THE colored people of America are going to their own papers in these days for the news and for their guidance in thinking. These papers are coming to them from a score of Northern cities—Boston, New York, Philadelphia, Chicago, Cleveland; they are coming to them from the great border cities —Baltimore, Washington, Cincinnati, St. Louis; they are coming to them from every Southern city. Wherever in all the land there is a considerable Negro population there is a Negro newspaper. Little Rock has four, Louisville five, Indianapolis six, New York City ten; the State of Georgia has nine, Mississippi nineteen, Illinois eleven, California seven.

To these numbers must be added the publications of churches, societies, and schools. For example, Mississippi has eleven religious weeklies, eight school periodicals, and two lodge papers, making a total, with the nineteen newspapers, of forty periodicals. And all classes of these contain articles on racial strife, outcries against wrongs and persecutions. You cannot take up even a missionary review or a Sunday school quarterly without being confronted by such an outcry.

As for the prosperity of these periodicals there is abundant evidence. As for their influence the evidence is no less. The Negro seems to have newly discovered his fourth estate, to have realized the extraordinary power of his press. Mighty as the pulpit has been with him, the press now seems to be foremost. It is freer than the pulpit, and there is a peculiar authority in printer's ink. His newspaper is the voice of the Negro.

Into every town and village of the land, and into many a log cabin in the mountains, come the colored papers, from all parts of the country, and these papers are read, and passed from hand to hand, and re-read until they are worn out. What do these papers contain? What is their tone, their spirit? How do they report the happenings of the day—the lynchings of Negroes, the riots, or mob-assaults? What manner of

ix

editorial.comment do they make? What kind of cartoons do they contain? What instruction do they give their readers?

After some months of close perusal of dozens and scores of colored weeklies, published North, South, East, and West, it seemed to the present writer that it would be a service to the country to make a compilation from them that should fairly represent their contents, their presentation of the news, and their discussions and comments. That the Negro himself has this right to be heard in the court of the world will not be denied except by the hopelessly prejudiced and constitutionally unjust. We have too frequently heard foolish vaunts about "knowing the Negro," the context of such boasting invariably convicting the speaker of dangerous conceit and the harsh spirit of suppression. Those who would honestly seek to know the Negro must read his papers. It is in them the Negro speaks out with freedom, with sincerity, with justice to himself, for there he speaks as a Negro to Negroes, and he is aware that the white people do not so much as know of the existence of his papers.

To know the Negro do not quiz the cook in your kitchen, or the odd-job, all-service menial about your premises, or the local school-teacher or preacher. In general they will tell you what they know you wish to hear, or, on difficult matters, remain non-committal. To know the Negro do not fall foul of two or three publications of Chicago or New York: there are some pretty radical and rather bolshevistically inclined white papers, according to the Post Office Department, in those quarters. We do not regard them as representing White America. To know the Negro read his papers extensively, particularly those that issue from Atlanta, and Richmond, and Little Rock, and New Orleans, and Dallas, and Raleigh, and Louisville, and Chattanooga, and a score of other cities south of the Mason and Dixon Line, as well as those of the émigrés in the North. Read their editorials, their sermons and addresses, and their news items; read their reports of the proceedings of their congresses, conventions, and conferences, their petitions and resolutions; read their poems and stories and dramatic sketches; look at their cartoons. This thing I have been doing, assiduously, and, I trust, with an open mind and friendly disposition, since mid-summer, 1919. After the riot in our nation's capital it seemed to me that the Negro's version of the story, whatever it was, should be heard. The riots that followed, North and South, East and West, confirmed me in my purpose to get at that story and present it to the white public, if that public would accept it.

Obtaining a full list of colored papers and magazines, I applied to them for copies dating onward from July the first. My study table was soon heaped with copies of hundreds of publications. I made a selection of fifty-three, which, after much study, I judged to be the most representative, and subscribed for them. The extracts which constitute the body of this book are made, I may therefore say, from the entire range of current Negro publications, but in the main from the half hundred that seemed to be the ablest, most prosperous, most independent, and most representative. My list of quoted papers, however, numbers eighty, and I studied twice as many.

For the scope of the work, the range of topics dealt with in the excerpts, I refer the reader to the Table of Contents. But to indicate more completely the character of the work I will set down here the following notes:

A period of four months, from July 1 to November 1, is covered. For information on one or two topics I have gone beyond the latter date.

Only colored papers and magazines have been quoted, never any white paper or writer. With three exceptions only has anything been taken second-hand, and these are properly accredited.

A much larger use has been made of Southern papers than of Northern, for obvious reasons.

I have read and re-read my mass of clippings, sifted and resifted them, to reduce their bulk and to select the most typical on the various topics.

All comments, except purely explanatory ones, and all critical remarks have been refrained from. The reader is left to make his own judgments.

No editing except to correct obvious typographical errors has been done.

For every excerpt or article included ten of like character on the same topic have probably been left in my mass of clippings.

The selections are meant to sweep the whole gamut of expression as regards temper and tone from the mildest to the most vigorous. Whatever of "radicalism" and "dangerous tendency" the colored press of America exhibits may be learned from the following pages by all who care to know. Only the unimportant exception is to be made that from the

three or four Northern periodicals that have fallen under the
condemnation of certain Southern congressmen and the Post
Master General, I have not taken any extracts that would
prima facie convict them of bolshevism, for the obvious reason
that the white press has sufficiently displayed and exploited
this news.

In fairness to the colored papers I must state specifically
that it lay beyond the design of this compilation to attempt
a general exposition of their contents. Their great function as
public instructors of their people on all manner of subjects in
all the departments of life, could not here be exhibited. The
reader is, therefore, warned against concluding that he here
obtains a complete view from what was meant to present but
a comprehensive view of a single matter.

THE VOICE OF THE NEGRO

THE VOICE OF THE NEGRO

I. THE COLORED PRESS

1. Its Comments Upon Itself

"FIFTEEN years ago, it was the exceptional home that received its race newspaper each week; five years ago it was the average home; to-day, the average home receives not only one race periodical, but usually two or more, and the exceptional home, office, store, the schools and churches and libraries, receive from six to more than a score. This is PROGRESS; this is SUCCESS.

"But we have a long way to go. True, in thousands of instances, the remotest cabins in the distant hills receive their newspapers now, and the occupants read them religiously. Through the magnificent advantage of the Associated Negro Press, all important happenings of the race are known regularly in every section of the nation, and by all classes. But there are yet thousands of homes into which our newspapers must go; there are millions of dollars spent with firms that should be induced to advertise in our periodicals, in a spirit of reciprocity, and to enable publishers to meet the heavy expense of adequate publicity, as do the daily newspapers.

"IN THESE CRUCIAL DAYS OF THE ACID TEST, EVERY READER OF EVERY NEWSPAPER SHOULD MAKE HIMSELF, OR HERSELF, AN UNTIRING AGENT AND COMMITTEE OF ONE, TO SEE THAT THESE NEEDS ARE BROUGHT TO PASS. WE HAVE THE ENEMIES OF JUSTICE ON THE RUN, AND STEADY FIRE WILL BRING THEIR WATERLOO. ONWARD!"
—*The Associated Negro Press.*

"The Negro press was never more militant nor more wide awake for race progress than it is to-day. Our press is the people's natural spokesman, and its voice rings true. It is sane without being timid—radical without being a firebrand."—
The Freeman (Indianapolis), October 18.

1

"There was a time when the newspapers and magazines of the Race were regarded as jokes, or as a political asset around election times. Conditions have changed. The newspapers and magazines of the Race have become a real factor, not only in economic progress, but as a constant and faithful expression of the feelings and will of the people.

"These facts are further emphasized by the marvelous increase in circulation, and the advertising growth of all publications. Negro journalism is a field of opportunity, second to none in progress and possibilities."—*The Phoenix* (Ariz.) *Tribune,* September 6.

"The greatest influence in the Race to-day, the influence that is demonstrating, beyond question, aggressive and militant leadership, frank, fair, fearless, faithful—is the NEWSPAPERS! In the light of other days, the influence of our newspapers is amazingly hopeful. Under the banners of Justice and True Americanism, they are leading onward to mighty victories for the people. Their mighty voice of appeal for the things that are fair and right, is getting the ears of the thinking people of all Races, in America and the world at large. The fangs of prejudice are being loosened, and the wild-eyed haters of humanity, in all parts of the land, are becoming alarmed beyond measure. Many of their lifelong friends are deserting them, and joining the side of right; the evidence is found in Congress—at last; in the editorial expressions of the daily newspapers, North and South; in the testimony and action of public men who are now daring to speak their convictions; in the coöperative endeavors of sensible people of all groups to get together and give serious consideration—a thing which has really never been done before—to the problems of adjustment. In the light of these facts, there is hope ahead."—*The Boston Chronicle,* October 11.

"ON THE RIGHT TRAIL

The determination of Governor Robertson to appoint a commission to discuss a program for the improvement of race relations is the thing that should have been done a long time ago. There is no excuse for the two races living in the same country and in this state and still so distant in opinion. So much misunderstanding is the logical product of the ignorant system of separation. We mean this sort of separation, what apparent interest has the white newspaper editor in what the Negro editor says. The white editor positively ignores the opinion of the black man as expressed through the Negro journal. Year in and year out you may read the white journals of this state and you will get nothing that reflects the real psychology of the black man. The only thing that you may find in white journals is the exaggeration of his faults and the expression of some particular Negro who may happen to say what the white editor would want said.

"In this way the white editor accepts a grave responsibility. He bars the masses of his race from the real thought of the black man. He cuts out the approach to the only bridge that the white masses have to cross to the opinion of black folk that is really worth while; in fact the white newspaper REALLY HOLDS A MANDATORY OVER WHAT THE WHITE MASSES SHALL KNOW ABOUT THE NEGRO and in the handling of this great responsibility they have erred greatly.

"If you were to headline the crime of every white man who is red headed in the daily papers for six months, you would have the average citizen walking off the sidewalk, walking around all of the red headed people that they meet. Center on a particular class and say that this Red Headed man did this and this Red Headed woman did that and in six months you will have it in the minds of the average person that red headed people are vile and corrupt creatures.

"In the press of America, all that the Negro gets is headlines for his faults, 'BIG BURLY BLACK BRUTE DOES THIS AND HUGE BLACK NEGRO FIEND DOES THAT.' This is the advertisement and the only sort of introduction that the Negro daily gets to white masses. The slightest offense or infraction of the law is sufficient to put the black man on the front page.

"The Negro's real heart and virtue rarely ever is exposed to America. We have a right to proper representation before the bar of public opinion, but we have not had it. If this conference work of Governor Robertson is carried through to the point where it ought to be, there will come a change that will lift the black man in the estimation of those who do not know that we are at least human."—*The Black Dispatch* (Oklahoma City), October 10.

"The People want and are demanding good newspapers, real newspapers and magazines. The Race not only is reading but is reading with a growing judgment of the quality of what is being read. Race people are thinking, and are seriously studying their problems and those of the nation as never before.

. . . .

"Circulation in all our newspapers, practically, has jumped from 100 to 300 per cent in the last five years. During the same period advertising patronage has jumped from 50 to 200 per cent."—*The Associated Negro Press.*

2. *Its Comments on the White Press*

A cartoon in *The Chicago Defender,* September 10, entitled "Fanning the Smoldering Embers," pictured its idea of the white press. A corpulent, bewhiskered, spectacled, gorilla-like white man, with pen above ear and a newspaper entitled "The Daily Prevaricator" protruding from his coat-tail pocket and exposing the full-page headline "Negro Rapes White Woman," is fanning with his hat some smoldering brands labeled "Race Hatred," "Washington Riots," "Chicago Riots," "Knoxville Riots." On this Frankenstein monster's coat was the label "Agitating White Press," and above his head was expressed his diabolically gleeful sentiment—"A little more and I'll have it blazing right."

This cartoon is the colored press's arraignment of the white press. It is the universal Negro view of the criminality of the white press. A typical brief protest must suffice:

"Every newspaper editor of our group in the country knows that the Associated Press, the leading news distributing service of the country, has carried on a policy of discrimination in favor of the whites and against the blacks, and is doing it daily now. The Associated Negro Press is in receipt of correspondence from editors in various sections of the country decrying the way in which the Associated Press writes its stories of happenings where Colored people are affected."—*The Wichita Protest,* October 31.

Such comments as this have appeared in almost every weekly newspaper in the country. Long editorials handle the subject vigorously. But something concrete and specific will be more to the point. Relative to an incident of the Washington riot, *The Crisis* printed the following exposé:

"The Riot-Mill

This is the way the white American press starts race riots: On August 5, the *Washington Post* published this account, on the third page, top of the column, toward the outer edge of the sheet. Notice the multiplicity of details and the attempt at an exact description of the alleged assailants. All the possible resources of "make-up" were brought to play. We present an exact photographic copy:

'ATTACKED BY NEGROES

Two Assailants Get Away

'Two squads of headquarters detectives, aided by reserves from the Ninth precinct, early to-day were searching houses and scouring fields in the neighborhood of Fifteenth and H streets northeast in an effort to apprehend two young negroes who shortly before 10 o'clock last night attacked Mrs. Minnie Franklin near the carnival tents on the old Union League ball grounds.

'While hundreds of merrymakers thronged the carnival tents Mrs. Franklin was subjected to treatment that left her hysterical and able to make but vague statements as to the affair. A partial description of the colored men was obtained from persons who saw them fleeing from the scene of the crime.

COVERED HER WITH PISTOL

'Mrs. Franklin, who is 37 years old and the wife of Edward S. Franklin, of 1361 K street southeast, is understood to have been with a companion at the carnival. They had walked away from the main tent, but were still in the radius of light from gasoline torches, when the two negroes appeared. One of them cowed Mrs. Franklin with a revolver.

'Several minutes later she staggered to the entrance of the grounds and related what had occurred. The police were communicated with at once, as was Casualty Hospital. Mrs. Franklin was removed to the institution, where she was treated and questioned by detectives. Later she was taken to her home, where her husband and children were apprised of the attack.

LAWLESS ELEMENT IN CROWD

'A special detail from the Ninth precinct has been stationed at the carnival since its inauguration, but until last night no disorder had been reported from the grounds. It is known, however, that a lawless element, both white and colored, had been attracted to the 'free-for-all' scene of jollity.

'The description of the negroes flashed from headquarters reads as follows:

"Look out for two colored men, 5 feet 3 or 4 inches in height; brown skin, 23 to 25 years old; wearing white shirts, no coats, tan or yellow caps."

* * *

"On August 16, this tiny article appeared tucked away on page 5, in the middle of the first column, on the inner edge. Need we comment?

'CALLS ASSAULT A "STORY"

Mrs. Franklin's Charge Against Two Negroes Dropped by Police

'In a statement to headquarters detectives last night, Mrs. Minnie Franklin, of 1361 K street southeast, declared, according to her questioners, including Detectives Vermillion, Embrey, O'Brien and Bradley, that her story of having been attacked Thursday night near Fifteenth and H streets northeast by two negroes was a fabrication.

'Mrs. Franklin first was interrogated by Mrs. Mina C. Van Winkle, head of the woman's bureau. The case has been dropped.' "

. . . .

The white press's responsibility for the Omaha riot was declared throughout the colored press. A few typical utterances follow:

"As early as last June the Omaha branch of the National Association for the Advancement of Colored People held a meeting protesting against remarks of the chief of police in which he seemed to hold the entire colored population responsible for the acts of a few Negro criminals. At that meeting resolutions were passed deploring the tendency of newspapers to emphasize by glaring headlines the race of suspected assailants in cases of crime attributed to colored men.

"The same thing was done in our Denver papers last week. It said: 'U. S. Troops Ordered to Shoot Negroes,' 'Race Riot at Gary,' 'Negro Rapes White Woman,' 'Negroes Plan to Kill Whites in South,' and 'Negro Uprising.' All these glaring headlines were made to discredit the Negro in the Community in which he lives. At the same time, discourage him. It has a tendency to heat our enemies and cool our friends and the Negro in all parts of the United States pays dearly, even for the slightest racial misunderstanding. The Negro must keep his ear close to the ground."—*The Denver Star,* October 11.

"A Word to the Press

"The Monitor has frequently called the attention of the Omaha Daily News and the Omaha Daily Bee to the danger they were inviting by their sensational headlines and featuring of alleged crimes by Negroes. Now that this policy has borne such bitter fruit we appeal to you, Mr. Polcar, and to you, Mr. Rosewater, to desist from this policy and practice. In the light of recent occurrences is this asking too much?"— *The Monitor* (Omaha), October 12.

"A large number of white southerners driven by the same economic force which brought colored men here, also migrated to northern states, Nebraska getting its full quota. They have made things just as unpleasant for the colored population here as has been their wont in the south. It was pointed out that any number of southern whites are employed on the staffs of the northern dailies, and these reporters and re-write men, it is alleged, spare no pains to distort facts and to picture the colored man as the worst type. This tended to inflame the minds of the people here and as a result they were turned overnight, as it were, into beasts bearing human form."—*The East Tennessee News* (Knoxville), October 16.

The trouble in Phillips County, Arkansas, had, according to all accounts in both presses—though the two presses differed widely—an entirely different and more alarming origin than any riot that had hitherto occurred. The colored press's explanation will be given in the chapter on riots. It quite generally ridiculed from the start the idea of a Negro uprising in Arkansas to massacre the whites. All over the land the colored papers are arraigning their neighboring white papers for incendiary headlines and articles, false in statement and malicious in design.

The following news item, taken from *The New York Age*, November 1, but found in numerous weeklies, concerns a particular grievance of the colored people—arrest on mere suspicion or general description:

"KILLING OF POLICEMAN USED AS INCENDIARY TEXT

Abortive Effort so Far

(Special to THE NEW YORK AGE.)

Des Moines, Iowa.—That the white daily press is an active agent in the stirring up of race troubles was shown here recently in the abortive attempts of the Des Moines' papers to stir the whites to rioting pitch, following the killing of McCarthy, a policeman.

"The crime was charged to a 'tall, dark Negro,' and every colored man answering to that description was picked up by the police officers. When one man, who was thought to be the one wanted, was arrested, the papers carried the fact in glaring headlines that spread across the page, and declared that angry mobs were gathering, when, as a matter of fact, there had been no demonstration of any sort.

"Pictures of the widow, with her seven children, were used, and every article published had some insidious sentiment tending to anger the whites. Finally, after several days of this newspaper propaganda, a small crowd of the lower element of whites did gather near the police station, but the better class of whites became active and the police authorities, after a change in the department had been made, soon cleared up the situation.

. . . .

"Strong efforts are being made to induce the white editors to cease the vicious propaganda of which they have the directing force and it can be seen that the whites are not so much inclined toward barbaric action as formerly."

3. Radicalism and Conservatism

Manifestly these are relative terms which on different lips mean different things. That we may get the Negro's point of view on this subject, which is fundamental, I will present two or three utterances:

"Our object in saying what we have said about the Negro and radicalism is to combat the propaganda that the Negro is a 'dangerous radical' because he is demanding the common fundamental rights that are accorded to all other citizens of the country."—*The New York Age.*

"RADICALISM

We used to think that certain of our leading men who continually harped upon and protested against discrimination and injustice were entirely 'too radical;' that they ought to go quietly and modestly about their own personal affairs and by the acquisition of property and education make themselves worthy of better treatment; that if they were denied the right to occupy property owned by them in a desirable neighborhood, they purchase property elsewhere and by their own acts improve that neighborhood. And there are lots of Colored people who think that now.

"But we have long since changed our views upon the subject. We think differently now. We really doubt if it is possible to be too radical in one's opposition to race hatred, discrimination and injustice.

"Radicalism does things. Be sure your cause is just and be as radical as you can. You cannot be too radical in a righteous cause."—*The Wisconsin Weekly Blade* (Madison), quoted by *The Crusader* (New York).

The following editorial paragraph is a splendid example of that cautious type of utterance which cannot convict the writer of "exciting race prejudice":

"A Better Civilization is more needed now in wise action of
all the people of this country that the good old way and
times may come back to us. There has been too much com-
promising all down the line and now we are facing the time
that we must take courage to say yes or no and stick to the
right forever more. God gave us to the world, so let us honor
the gift by standing for God's best, then comes good peace
and rest."—*The City Times* (Galveston, Tex.), November 1.

Words will therefore be judged differently. From a little,
old-fashioned, four-page paper published in Portsmouth, Va., I
take the following editorial:

"MUCH TO FIGHT FOR

This is the country of our birth, the land upon which we
grew, the people with whom we came into contact from our
first introduction to America, and it is here our parents lived,
toiled and died, and in this soil their bones are interred; it is
here the chains of slavery fell from our limbs and we started
on the upclimb.

"It is here we got our first knowledge of the Bible and
Jesus Christ; it is here we have begun to take shape as other
human beings along the lines of advanced civilization, and,
because that many of these things are too dear to be thrown
away or given away, we, to maintain them, have much to fight
for."—*The Vigil.*

Dangerous? Certainly not, if you are thinking of its power
to excite a riot. But if it be taken as the restrained and cautious utterance of a grief-burdened, grievance-harboring people,
patient but protesting under a sense of injustices and wrongs,
we need to be awakened to the tremendous danger of neglect-
ing to heed it.

Some papers evidently think silence the only safe policy.
Among these papers, *The Gate City Bulletin* (Denison, Texas),
is apparently to be classed, as one may perceive by the following editorial, October 25:

"WHY WE DON'T

This paper has been criticised by some folks because it does not carry much news about the American Sensation (lynching) and because it refuses to devote its columns to the general fight put on by colored editors.

"Well, about the only thing a fellow can do when he's tied hand and foot is to cuss (unless he's gagged) and my latest conclusion is that cursing only keeps the big show going while he, the untameable beast, remains caged."

Hardly a paper can be found, however slight in appearance, but raises its voice to protest against conditions, unjust treatment, outrageous wrongs, and to make demands. The unanimity is all but absolute.

At the head of its editorial page *The Memphis Times* carries this pronouncement of principle:

"The Memphis Times was established by S. W. Broome, March 9, 1918. It stands for progress, reform and the highest development of the race on all lines; speaks out against injustice and corruption; it uses its influence for equal rights to all. 'All men up and no man down.' It is a factor for social uplift, mental, moral and spiritual development, as well as commercial and financial."

In justification of its moderation of tone it speaks thus:

"THERE IS POWER IN TRUTH

The Negro newspapers of the country have endeavored to be fair in giving out the news to the public in general. They have stuck to the line of facts and truth. Plain truth has been the watchword in all matters with which they have to deal. Often our findings, through careful and patient investigation, have differed very materially from that of the white press in some sections of the country. Our findings and reports have generally come after excitement is over and communities have gotten back into joint and conditions are normal. The editors have been very careful not to give out news until true facts could be obtained. We have not to appear radical, but truthful, because we believe that truth is powerful and coupled with right she always will finally prevail.

"Our finding in the Arkansas trouble differs so widely from the first report that we have refrained from report, and this often wisdom dictates, for there are times when even truth itself will hurt, and there are times when even our best friends among the whites must not be embarrassed and hindered in their efforts to bring about a better day—we must be patient, we must wait on God, we must wait till truth can get a hearing—she is powerful and will prevail."

The difference, wherever there is any, between Northern and Southern papers, may be exemplified by the two following extracts:

"Du Bois maintained in the June *Crisis* 'that we believe that the crushing of the monstrous pretensions of the military caste of Germany was a duty so pressing and tremendous that it called for the efforts of every thoughtful American.' With this sentiment, we take sharp issue. We were not at any time interested in the reactionary militarist government of Germany. We desired to see it crushed, as crushed it would be undoubtedly with the rising tide of German Socialism and German democracy. But as it was, we did not for one moment regard it as important as crushing the southern bourbon caste system of peonage in the United States. The Huns of Georgia are far more menacing to Negroes than the Huns of Germany. The Huns of Alsace have never threatened the Negro's life, liberty, and property like the Huns of Alabama. The Huns of Lorraine are as shining angels of light compared to the Huns of Louisiana. No barbarians of Turkey could ever be compared with the howling, Dervish-dancing barbarians of Tennessee."—*The Guardian* (Boston). Report of an address.

"We are told, and we read it for ourselves, too, that the North is still inviting our people to come up and fill the vacancies made by the foreigners daily. And of course the invitation will be accepted more readily the more the law is laid aside for Hunism.

"Our good white friends of the South had better awake and demand a stop, else the North will grow in prosperity upon the wickedness or Hunism of the South."—*The Southern Indicator,* Columbia, S. C. Editorial.

It was in a paper published in the Black Belt I saw this sentence, which by itself constituted an editorial:

"Hellish Huns—Barbarous Bourbons, one and the same—synonyms."

The Dallas Express is not of the feebler sort. It is a prosperous-looking, sixteen-page paper. It calls itself conservative. A declaration placed by its founder at the head of its editorial page reads as follows:

The Dallas Express has never hoisted the white feather, neither has it been disgraced by the yellow streak. It is not affiliated with the flannel mouth. It is a plain, every day, sensible, conservative newspaper, which trims no sail to catch the passing breeze; flies no doubtful flag. It professes a patriotism as broad as our country. Its love of even handed justice covers all the territory occupied by the human race. This is pretty high ground, but we live on it and are prospering. Boys of the press come up and stand with us. This ground is holy.—W. E. KING.

Notwithstanding this self-description if many of its editorials be not radical it would be difficult to find what should fall under that characterization—"radical" as going to the *root* of the matter. The following editorial, November 1, will serve as an example of its "plain, everyday, sensible, conservative" style:

"When the South unblushingly asserts that it knows the Negro best and is best prepared to deal with the race problem, it again grapples with a responsibility scarcely less formidable than that so lightly assumed by its ancestors, who dared again to resurrect the institution of chattel slavery after Christianity had decreed that it should be forever banished from among the sons of men.

"Since Democracy has been established for the world through the shedding of rivers of blood and the sacrifice of millions of human lives, must any portion of this great nation which carried the fight for democracy to the very gates of militarism and autocracy now hesitate in applying this great principle without reservation to every class and race throughout its broad dominions? Will the South assume such a responsibility in the solution of this most vexing race problem? Shall the mistake of her ancestors that brought ruin to the fairest portion of this great Republic be repeated by the present generation? Shall the American people learn through the South that the protection and prosperity vouchsafed by democracy is a myth and can be denied to any portion of the American people who are unable to secure justice through the influence of public opinion? If justice and opportunity can be denied the Negro it can be denied any other race or class of people if public opinion should so shift as to permit it. In securing justice for the Negro you secure the perpetuation of justice for the whole American people. If justice be denied the Negro it is thereby denied to the American people because the Negro is part and parcel of this people."

The articles within on the various topics will reveal, according to each reader's standard, what papers are radical and what conservative. But that the Colored press is not to be deterred from agitating for fear of being accused of radicalism there is abundant evidence.

That there is a considerable portion of the colored press that advocates extreme measures—retaliation, blood for blood, life for life—cannot be questioned. A few representative utterances will be quoted.

That there are Socialist editors among the several hundred in our country, that there may be at most three who advocate something like a Soviet form of government, may also be true. That a considerable number are violent in denunciation of our Government, and particularly of the present Administration, is what any reader of the papers of any group or party in any country might expect in coming to the Afro-American papers in view of our lynching record, our proscription and segregation principles, and our sweeping discriminations on account of color.

The Boston Guardian has its columns open to extreme radicalism, and almost every week reports an address or sermon of the character indicated by the following extract from a column of like utterances:

"AN EYE FOR AN EYE IS DOCTRINE TAUGHT BY RADICAL LEADER

(By Associated Negro Press)

BOSTON, Mass., July 28.—The Rev. Dr. M. A. N. Shaw of the 12th Baptist church, Shawmut avenue and Madison street, delivered a fiery address yesterday afternoon from his pulpit on the present and future status of his Race in America. The gathering was called as an 'all fraternal' meeting, delegations from Colored Masons, Odd Fellows, Elks, Knights of Pythias and the Love and Charity lodges being invited to attend.

"The recent lynching at Laurel, Miss., gave point to the pastor's discourse, and he described the hanging, burning and disemboweling of Mary Turner, because, he said, she had said that if she knew the names of the lynchers of her husband she would turn them over to the police.

"'We have got, as a people,' he said, 'to insist that we be lynched no more, that acts attended with savagery that would put to shame the most atrocious acts by the Germans in time of war, and practices by southern aristocrats in time of peace, shall cease. The Negro who hesitates to stop the wholesale butchery of his race should himself be lynched.'"

The editor of *The Guardian* is quoted in his own paper, August 2, as having said in an address in Palace Theatre, New York, that unless the white Americans do the right thing they will "find out that when they taught the colored boys to fight they started something they won't be able to stop."

The audience of 2000 colored people was reported by *The New York Age* to have unanimously endorsed by resolution "the method of force and violence as a means of attaining their ends."

From a regular contributor to *The Cleveland Gazette*, Rev. Wm. A. Byrd, comes this article, which is representative of his contributions and the attitude of that paper:

"THE MILITIA IN RACE RIOTS

Dr. Wm. A. Byrd Castigates 'Sycophant Black Men'

In all of the riots that have occurred, the municipalities have called out the militia to quell them. Only white soldiers have been called on. In every instance the sympathy of the militia was with the rioting whites. Colored people have had to fight both the lawless white mob and the militia. Then, too, the soldiers have invariably gone to the section of the cities where colored people live. They have searched every colored man to take away from him his gun or means of defense, but white cowards have been left untouched. If municipalities desire justice done they should ask for soldiers of both races. The bitter spirit now extant in this country, since the war, is due very largely to the hostility between white and colored soldiers. In the south, white soldiers are worse than white civilians. They cannot be trusted to maintain order by compelling both white and black rioters to live up to the same standard. As it is, colored people, to protect themselves, must give battle to soldiers. Too often these boys in uniform rejoice at the opportunity to kill colored men. The soldiery of the south is not one whit better than the citizenry of the south. The oath taken by the white soldier is of no more force than the oath taken by the white southern officer who is the leader of the mob. It is plain to the most casual observer that colored people are not rioting but are defending themselves against the hordes of white desperadoes. There is no propaganda afoot to dissuade white demons from perpetuating their riots but sycophant black men, some in high places, are calling upon colored men to desist from rioting. These dastardly cowards are better dead than alive! Colored men are simply defending their lives and homes. We say to them—continue defending them until the last man falls and then let the women take up the fight! The Knoxville riot is simply one of many that are coming in the south. Southern 'crackers' were at the foundation of the riots in Washington and Chicago. They failed to overawe the colored men in those cities and now the attempt is to take it into the south where they hope to be more successful. In this they are sadly mistaken. Colored men in no portion of this country will run, unless it is some of the cringers in high places who are living off the life-blood of the colored men who are giving standing and backbone to the race. Those Negro bishops and other sycophants that called upon colored men to be quiet while white villains were destroying their homes, brutalizing their women, robbing them of manhood and reducing the entire race to serfdom; we repeat, those bishops should be driven out of the country. They are unworthy of respect. Ireland in its fight for liberty has its clergy in the front leading! American Negroes in their fight for life and liberty, have their clergy skulking and cringing, making appeals to them to continue as slaves. Such a clergy does not deserve the respect of savages. We believe in order and law. We desire all men to live up to this standard. But we demand of the colored race to protect themselves at all hazards! Gentlemen, you are not rioting, but are doing your duty. It is the duty of municipalities where rioting is, to force white men to respect the law. What a contrast! White ministers are not rushing into print advising their people to be law-abiding and orderly. Judges and officers of the law are not appealing to white men to desist from mobbing colored people. The militia is sent for when they see colored men 'mopping up the white trash.' But Negroes of every shade are giving advice to colored men 'to stop.' Don't heed the infamous cowards! Protect your homes. Don't start anything but when something is started make it hot for them and finish it!"

From *The Journal and Guide* (Norfolk, Va.), August 2, I take the last half of an editorial, as follows:

"THE NATIONAL DISGRACE AND SHAME

Two phases of the Washington race rioting are worthy of more than a momentary reflection. The soldiers and sailors who undertook to lynch Joseph Collins, whom the police had released from custody because they had no evidence upon which to convict him of criminal assault, put themselves in the position of knowing more about it than the Federal Trial Judge. For which they should be made to answer to the civil as well as to the military and naval authorities. If not, why not?

"Having failed to lynch Collins the lynchocrats in uniforms started out to lynch any Afro-American they should come across. This sword worked both ways. It aroused the mob spirit in the District of Columbia; and the blacks answered the challenge man for man and life for life. This must not have been expected. It certainly was surprising. White enthusiasm in the lawless slaughter began to freeze as soon as the blacks began to shoot and cut to kill; as they began on Monday to do. At last inside information, the jails contained more blacks than whites, but the hospitals contained quite as many whites as blacks.

"White folks don't like cold steel any more than black folks. The outcome of the rioting at Washington, and at Longview, Texas, which had a race riot and martial law while the Washington riot was in progress, is that the black masses driven to desperation by white mobs have reached the conclusion that the only way left to them is to meet white mob lawlessness with black mob lawlessness.

"It is a National disgrace and shame that any part of the citizenship of the Republic should be compelled to meet force with force in defense of life and property; but not since the Ku-Klux Klan lawlessness began in the Reconstruction era, forty-five years ago, have the States or the National government given Afro-American citizens the least protection of life and property from mob lawlessness, some 3,000 of them having been murdered and burned without due process of law; women as well as men have been so murdered, mutilated and burned. If the determination of those whom the Nation and the States leave to be dealt with by lynchocrats, to give their tormentors measure for measure, a limb for a limb, a life for a life, does not arouse the National government and the States to enact appropriate legislation to stamp out mob law, the Nation will go to wreck and ruin, as it will be unable to survive the assaults of Radical Socialist Bombocrats and Lawless Lynchocrats. That much is written in the words of the town clerk of Ephesus, in pronouncing against moblawlessness, not quite two thousand years ago."

The *Challenge Magazine* (New York), October, consecrates the battle under a biblical name:

"LET US STAND AT ARMAGEDDON AND BATTLE FOR THE LORD

Negroes, Unite!

"Brutal oppression is sweeping over us like storm-swept tidal waves.

"There will be no mercy shown us because we are black, standing on the highways of the world, pleading for mercy. There will be no sympathy given except what we have always gotten from a small coterie of white men whose puny numbers make them, with us, easy victims for the stigmatizing, lawless crowd. They, too, have cried out with us like Sumner, and Philips, Lovejoy, Garrison, Beecher and John Brown, but their voices have been drowned with ours in a holocaust of slander and abuse.

"We are ignored by the President and lawmakers. When we ask for a full man's share they cry 'insolent.' When we shoot down the mobist that would burn our properties and destroy our lives, they shout 'Bolshevist.' When a white man comes to our side armed with the sword of righteousness and square dealing, they howl 'Nigger-lover and bastard.' If we take our grievances to Congress they are pigeon-holed, turned over to moth. We are abandoned, cast off, maligned, shackled, shoved down the hills towards Golgotha in 'The Land of the Free and the Home of the Brave.'

"Every day we are told to keep quiet.

"Only a fool will keep quiet if he is being robbed of his birthright. Only a coward will lie down and whine under the lash if he, too, can give back the lash.

"There is little pity from the strong for the one that is weak. There is no altruistic religion in the soul of the strong for dispensation among the weak. The only pity obtained is that obtained by superior strength.

"America hates, lynches, enslaves us not because we are black, but because we are weak. A strong, united Negro race will not be mistreated any more than a strong united Japanese race. It is always strength over weakness, might over right.

"But with education comes thought, with thought comes action; with action comes freedom.

"Read Read! Read! Then when the mob comes, whether with torch or with gun, let us stand at Armageddon and battle for the Lord."

The following editorials, quoted entire, will more adequately represent the present attitude of the colored press on the question of resistance to mob assaults:

"Let Us Reason Together

Brothers, we are on the Great Deep. We have cast off on the vast voyage which will lead to Freedom or Death. For three centuries we have suffered and cowered. No race ever gave Passive Resistance and Submission to Evil longer, more piteous trial. To-day we raise the terrible weapon of Self-Defense. When the murderer comes, he shall not longer strike us in the back. When the armed lynchers gather, we too must gather armed. When the mob moves, we propose to meet it with bricks and clubs and guns.

"But we must tread here with solemn caution. We must never let justifiable self-defense against individuals become blind and lawless offense against all white folk. We must not seek reform by violence. We must not seek Vengeance. 'Vengeance is Mine,' saith the Lord; or to put it otherwise, only Infinite Justice and Knowledge can assign blame in this poor world, and we ourselves are sinful men, struggling desperately with our own crime and ignorance. We must defend ourselves, our homes, our wives and children against the lawless without stint or hesitation; but we must carefully and scrupulously avoid on our own part bitter and unjustifiable aggression against anybody.

"This line is difficult to draw. In the South the Police and Public Opinion back the mob and the least resistance on the part of the innocent black victim is nearly always construed as a lawless attack on society and government. In the North the Police and the Public will dodge and falter, but in the end they will back the Right when the Truth is made clear to them.

"But whether the line between just resistance and angry retaliation is hard or easy, we must draw it carefully, not in wild resentment, but in grim and sober consideration; and when back of the impregnable fortress of the Divine Right of Self-Defense, which is sanctioned by every law of God and man, in every land, civilized and uncivilized, we must take our unfaltering stand.

"Honor, endless and undying Honor, to every man, black or

The Colored Press 21

white, who in Houston, East St. Louis, Washington and Chicago gave his life for Civilization and Order.

"If the United States is to be a Land of Law, we would live humbly and peaceably in it—working, singing, learning and dreaming to make it and ourselves nobler and better; if it is to be a Land of Mobs and Lynchers, we might as well die to-day as to-morrow.

> 'And how can man die better
> Than facing fearful odds
> For the ashes of his fathers
> And the temples of his gods?' "
> —The Crisis (New York), September.

"To My Dear Brethren and Friends:—

Permit me to say this word to you in this time of most serious anxiety. You have read of the riots in St. Louis, Philadelphia and Chester, Pennsylvania, during the Great World War, and in Washington and Chicago since its close. When the facts have been finally sifted they have always shown, without doubt, that the colored people did not start these riots. They were started by whites in every instance.

"If there are to be riots in the future I want to say to my people, let it be as it has been in the past, that you shall not be the instigators of them. It is to be the everlasting disgrace of these Northern cities, as it has been of certain Southern cities, that these riots have been started by whites, and that white policemen, who should be the first to uphold the law, have, in nearly every instance, assisted the mobs.

"Now is the time for all of us to keep our wits; to do nothing wrong which may be any excuse for riot. Let men and women go about their work quietly, attending to their business. Keep away from saloons, and places where there is gambling. More trouble starts in these places than anywhere else. Avoid arguments. Make no boasts. Make no threats. Attack no man or woman without due provocation, and under no circumstances hurt a child.

"Don't tell anybody what the Negroes are going to do to the whites. For we do not want war; we want peace. Our safety is in peace.

"Don't loaf in the streets; do not needlessly encounter gangs of white boys. A gang of boys from 15 to 20 years of age is usually irresponsible. A gang of young white toughs will delight to 'jump' a lone Negro, especially if they number eight or a dozen, and believe the Negro is unarmed, and it is foolish to give them the chance.

"In trading, as nearly as possible get the right change before paying your bill; know what you want. Where you can, trade with your own people, where you are not liable to get into a dispute. Don't go to white theaters, white ice cream places, white banks, or white stores, where you can find colored to serve you just as well. In other words, don't spend your hard-earned money where you are in danger of being beaten up.

"Don't carry concealed deadly weapons—it's against the law.

"Now I am not urging cowardice. I am urging caution—due caution. I am urging common sense. I am urging law and order.

"Protect your home, protect your wife and children, with your life if necessary. If a man crosses your threshhold after you or your family, the law allows you to protect your home even if you have to kill the intruder. Obey the law, but do not go hunting for trouble. Avoid it. Avoid it.

"Do not be afraid or lose heart because of these riots. They are merely symptoms of the protest of your entrance into a higher sphere of American citizenship. They are the dark hours before morning which have always come just before the burst of a new civic light. Some people see this light and they provoke these riots, endeavoring to stop it from coming. But God is working. Things will be better for the Negro. We want full citizenship ballot, equal school facilities and everything else. We fought for them. We will have them; we must not yield. The greater part of the best thinking white people, North and South, know we are entitled to all we ask. They know we will get it. In their hearts they are for us, though they may fear the lower element who are trying to stir up trouble to keep us from getting our rights. But they will fail just as they failed to keep us from our freedom. God is with us. They cannot defeat God.

"So I say to you: stand aside, stand prepared, provoke no riot; just let God do His work. He may permit a few riots in order to force the Negroes closer together. He lets the hoodlums kill a few in order to teach the many that we MUST GET TOGETHER. But he does not mean that we shall be defeated—if we trust Him. Let us learn the lesson He is teaching us.

"Remember a riot may break out in any place. Let pastors

caution peace, prayer and preparedness. Let us provoke no trouble. Let us urge our congregations to keep level heads, and do nothing that is unlawful.

Yours in Christian bonds,

R. R. WRIGHT, JR."

Editor of *The Christian Recorder* (Philadelphia).

Self-defense is applauded and advocated, I believe, by the entire colored press, with one exception. *The Western Review* (Sacramento) advises non-resistance. But this fact of practical unanimity in recommending self-defense when assailed is perfectly consistent with a general temperateness of tone—a temperateness that lacks nothing of resoluteness of purpose.

Most of the colored papers declare their purposes or principles in mottoes placed about their name on the front page. Some are as follows: *The Pittsburg American* has: "Loyalty, Fraternity, Equality—Christianity, Opportunity, Liberty: An American Newspaper for Americans." *The Black Dispatch* (Oklahoma) has: "Progress," "Truth," "Light" on the three coaches of its express train, "Faith" emblazoned ahead, "Onward to the Heights" trumpeted by an angel above, and these declarations on the margins: "A paper with a policy," and "We stand for the right of the voice of men to be heard in their own government; for a Democracy that is an actuality not ritualistic." *The Fort Worth Star* has, "Equal Rights to All: Special Privileges to None." *The Colorado Statesman* has the Angel of Justice holding aloft in one hand the scales and in the other a broken chain; one of the columns of her temple is inscribed, "Labor shall be Free," and another, "Race, Country, Party"; at her feet are pictured the products and processes of all manner of toil. *The Raleigh Independent* has, "Independent in All Things: Neutral in Nothing."

II. THE NEW ERA

1. *The New Negro and the Old*

THAT the reactions of the Negro to the World War and to the discussion of the Treaty and the League have been strong must have been manifest to all. It is in his nature to react strongly to such influences. A new era and a new Negro are the results, according to his papers. The several aspects of this new era and of the new spirit shaping it will be set forth, as the Negro himself understands it, in this section.

An editorial in *The Broad Ax* (Chicago), September 6, points out some important distinctions between the old era and the new:

"We are living in a grand and awful time. The yesterdays are gone forever. . . .

"This bent and twisted form [of the bowing, kow-towing Negro] grew out of the innocent nature of the old Uncle Mose, Uncle Tom, and Aunt Betty, who were all right at heart and good as people ever were in Bible days, but, it has left its hurt in the blood. Show every one the proper respect due them, but if they don't show to you that Golden Rule spirit, let them alone: Republican, Democrat, Christian or Sinner.

"We have as a people given too much of our zeal to politics, and vastly more of our substance for the church. Both of these we have helped to develop to the successful point. The politician is on his way to something, the preacher is trying to point you to something, but this era ushers in a spirit to lay hold on something tangible.

"The economic principle and the spirit of commerce is the neglected child we long have failed to nourish. These principles, Economy and Industry, are the very foundations of the universe."

The going of the Old Negro is the subject of many editorials of which the following is an example:

"The Old Negro Goes: Let Him Go In Peace

The Old Negro and his futile methods must go. After fifty years of him and his methods the Race still suffers from lynching, disfranchisement, Jim Crowism, segregation and a hundred other ills. His abject crawling and pleading have availed the Cause nothing. He has sold his life and his people for vapid promises tinged with traitor gold. His race is done. Let him go.

"The New Negro now takes the helm. It is now OUR future at stake. Not his. His future is in the grave. And if the New Negro, imbibing the spirit of Liberty, is willing to suffer martyrdom for the Cause, then certainly the very least that the Old Negro can do is to stay in the background for his remaining years of life or to die a natural death without in his death struggles attempting to hamper those who take new means to effect ends which the Old Leaders throughout fifty years were not able to effect.

"Can the Old Leaders deny that there is more wholesome respect for the Negro following the race riots in Washington, Chicago, Knoxville and other places than there was before those riots and when there were only lynchings and burnings of scared Negroes and none of the fear in the white man's heart that comes from the New Negro fighting back? They cannot deny it, so let them go their way. The future is the New Negro's. It should have come to us safeguarded. But the Old Leaders have failed ignobly. Ours now is the task of safeguarding that future and of giving it to our children secured for all time. For us the future and all the great tasks that lie ahead. For the Old Leader *Requiescat in Pace!"—* The Crusader (New York), October.

2. New Leadership

The new era calls for new leaders. Few are the colored papers that have not expressed themselves decisively on this subject, demanding firmness, courage, manliness and aggressiveness in those who presume to lead, and denouncing compromise and cowardice. Radical leadership is sometimes decried; conservative, sane leadership is usually commended: but the same full list of demands for justice and privilege is the platform of all.

The People's Pilot (Richmond, Va.), in its August number, editorially describes the several schools of leadership and names the one now predominant.

The article will be quoted as representing, not by any means the entire Negro press, but a considerable portion of it, especially several of the newer papers, including *The People's Pilot* itself. Very many other papers follow the older school of leaders, of the Hampton and Tuskegee type.

"A League of Leaders

There are, in America, three Schools of Negro Leadership. "1. The Booker T. Washington idea embraced by Hampton and Tuskegee—the idea that Negroes were created to fit only into a niche of servitude and labor in this great American body politic. 2. The DuBoisian idealism demanded by intellectual statesmanship. This school claims that the Negro is the crux of world democracy—unless he is freed the rest of mankind must also remain enslaved to some form of detestable autocracy or abortive democracy. Its method is one of publicity and agitation. 3. The Kelly Miller Medium espoused by the followers of Dean Miller of Howard University. This School lost its cue when the so-called two extremes disappeared. The influence of the first extreme died with the death of the great apostle of Industrialism. That incident along with the coming of the war brought the School of DuBois into the ascendency.

". . . The Negro Press and every useful agent for Negro uplift should say one say and do one do. Let us have the 'League of Leaders,' 'Close Ranks' among ourselves. Lay aside our various jealousies, for the time being, and wisely use the greatest opportunity that has ever come to our race in America and the world. The white man has vanquished his enemy in the World War by united action and has turned to devour the darker peoples who helped him to conquer his foe. We must do as he did and overcome him or let him treat us as he has treated his enemy."

3. *Race Traitors*

The complement of this approval of courage and fidelity in leadership is the contempt poured out by the colored press, with

absolute unanimity, upon every act of race betrayal, race dis-
loyalty, and cowardice. The language of anathema is strained to
the limit for the adequate castigation of tale-bearers and lick-
spittles, the cringing, hat-in-hand tribe, the Brutuses and Bene-
dict Arnolds.

The following extracts from an editorial in *The Fort Worth
Hornet,* October 25, suggest an explanation of the compromis-
ing spirit and hypocritical speeches of a portion of the race:

"Beggar Leaders

Many Negro men throughout the United States and the
southern states in particular have felt called upon in the last
few months to rush into the newspapers, purporting to speak
for 12,000,000 Colored people and dealing out some of the most
disgusting rot that we have ever been forced to read. The
time will come in the south when men, white men, will refuse
to encourage these so-called and self-appointed Negro beggars
to work and play a game of deception. Most of these miserable hypocrites throw around them an orphan home cloak;
or a church cloak, or a purposed industrial Negro school cloak,
where girls are to be taught cooking and the boys farming."

This from *The Mobile Forum,* October 11, is of like im-
port. The quoted paragraphs conclude a long editorial:

"False Leadership

True leaders are men who at all times, according to their
light, stand unflinchingly for the interests committed to their
care and for the greatest good to the largest number. They
are above quibbling and jealousies and deception and self-
serving. No opportunity for selling out the community's interest to secure personal aggrandizement or material property can
tempt them to swerve from the path of honor and right. They
are men who cannot be bought.

"In times like these we need men who are true—leaders who
will place the people's welfare above every other consideration.
Only men of strength and stamina and of unyielding character
where right is involved are thus equipped and dependable.
God grant such men to us. All others will fail utterly and
ignobly, as they should."

Of the milder type of editorial denunciation the following may be taken as an example. It is from *The Newport News Star*, October 3:

"Any Negro who says that he is satisfied to be let alone with his broken political power, his miserable Jim Crow restrictions, his un-American segregation, his pinched and emasculated democracy, and his blood-curdling inquisition of lynching, simply lies. He lies basely. He knows himself he lies, and the white man knows he lies. He does not fool anybody. He disgusts his friends, and earns only the contempt of those whose favor he seeks to win. He assumes this contemptible attitude, not because he is feeble-minded, however, but because he has a white liver. He is an arrant coward and a traitor besides."

So through two additional paragraphs of scathing denunciation it continues, giving explanations, incidentally, of such cowardly treason.

The Washington [D. C.] *Bee* of October 18 speaks thus editorially of a set of "colored traitors" in Georgia:

"Colored Traitors

Is it true that two colored, so-called representative men from the State of Georgia, have been employed by certain white men in the South to come to Washington and appear before the Committee on Interstate Commerce and oppose the Madden bill to abolish 'Jim Crow' cars in the South? Is it true that there exists among colored Americans, at this time, traitors? Is it true that the so-called intelligent colored man is becoming so base and treacherous to his race? Well, this is the rumor that has been circulated in and around the Senate and House of Representatives of the United States.

"The Bee is surprised, because it has been of the opinion that colored informers and traitors died with the reconstruction of the South. The young colored man at this time can be trusted, but the matured colored politician of the old school must be looked upon with suspicion. There are twelve million colored Americans in the United States, and of that number there may be a thousand colored traitors of the old school of politicians. It is the young colored Americans who are defending the rights and the liberties of their people, and the old school politician is the dangerous element in society."

4. "Good-By, Black Mammy"

Another but not different view of this new temper of the Negro is afforded in what he has to say regarding the Southern white man's profession of friendship. He is repudiating that friendship on the terms on which it is offered. He is refusing to accept kindness in lieu of justice. It has long been the custom, according to the colored papers, for the Southern white man to make a creditable asset of his affection for some dear old black "mammy," and this or that "auntie" or "uncle." To the new Negro this profession makes no appeal whatsoever. It does not touch the question of his demands.

From *The Christian Index* (Jackson, Tenn.), July 31, I take a paragraph of a reported address by C. H. Tobias, Secretary of the International Committee of the Y. M. C. A.:

"The sentiment surrounding the old tradition of the 'Black Mammy' and the South must now be changed so as to meet the conditions surrounding the sons and grandsons of 'Black Mammy.' It was not 'Black Mammy' who responded one half million strong to the call to fight for the preservation of world democracy, but it was 'Black Mammy's' sons and grandsons, and however much the South may revere the memory of 'Black Mammy,' the attitude of the South towards the black man must take into account the aspirations for citizenship with all that the word connotes on the part of the younger generation of Negroes."

But the full aspect of the matter with all that it involves, which on consideration is much, is set forth editorially in *The Southwestern Christian Advocate* (New Orleans):

"Good-by Black Mammy

Our southern white friends play up to great effect their affections for the picturesque and lovable character commonly known as 'Black Mammy' who formerly held a very conspicuous place in our Southern life. [A story is here taken from *The Wesleyan Christian Advocate* of four Southern born white gentlemen acting as honorary pall-bearers at a black mammy's funeral.]

"Those who do not know the intricacies of race relations in the South would be most likely misled in the reading of these paragraphs and wonder why with such feeling as indicated in this editorial remark there is so much restlessness and hostility between the races. In the first place, the pall bearers at the funeral of this 'faithful servant,' who were four Southern born white gentlemen, would have dropped stone dead before they would have acted as pall bearers at the funeral of one of the faithful law-abiding Negroes, who, the Wesleyan Christian Advocate says, can trust the Southern people to treat them fairly and justly,—if this faithful law-abiding Negro did not sustain a subservient, truckling and subordinate position to these four Southern white gentlemen.

"The Wesleyan is dead right when it says that the 'Black Mammy' would not give a penny for more rights than she has had and her social relation with the white people is as cordial and fair as she could wish. All that we can say is that that is the attitude of the 'Black Mammy' as far as outside appearances are concerned. There were those of this class who were absolutely satisfied with their subordinate relations but when they get out from under the roofs of their master their attitude is entirely different. The 'Black Mammy' however is going and we bid her an affectionate good-by and a long farewell."

III. THE NEGRO'S REACTION TO THE WORLD WAR

1. *Valor and Sacrifice*

In *The Planet* (Richmond, Va.), August 30, the Reverend R. C. Ransom, editor *A. M. E. Review* (Philadelphia), is quoted as having described in an address to the Order of St. Luke at Richmond the passing of the old order in the following language:

" ' . . . And God shall wipe away all tears from their eyes . . . neither shall there be any more pain; for the former things are passed away . . . Behold all things are new.' And I say with John on Patmos, "Old things have passed away." ' They began to pass away soon after France and Germany locked arms while in the first battle of the Marne. Old things began to pass away in the second battle of the Marne. Old things passed away when Roberts and Johnson on the field of No Man's Land shed their blood in the cause of Liberty. Old things began to pass away when four hundred thousand black men joined with the other race on No Man's Land— and when they return this nation must understand that 'old things have passed away.'

"In speaking of the old order of things in relation to the former so called 'old type' of Negro of antebellum and civil war days, Mr. Ransom said, 'Between us and that Negro are lined up sixty thousand of the St. Luke Order. Between us and that Negro are thousands of doctors and thousands of lawyers and thousands of teachers and bankers and thousands of educated men and women from colleges and universities and high schools.' 'Old things have passed away.' "

The following concise summary of the record of heroism achieved by Negro troops in the World War was widely published:

"ARE YOU AWARE that a Negro Was the First American to Receive the Croix de Guerre with Palm and Gold Star? That

Three Negro Regiments and several battalions and companies were cited and had their flags decorated for valorous conduct? That Negroes Placed for the First Time in artillery and signal corps units won high distinction? That Negroes in the early part of the war held 20 per cent of all territory assigned to Americans? That the Negro Army was the healthiest on record? That out of 45,000 Negroes engaged in battle only 9 were taken prisoners? Negroes Fought to the Death rather than submit to captivity. That the Negroes established a record for continuous service in the trenches—191 days?"

As for the actual part played by the Negro in the World War, as for the courage and fighting qualities of the troops, it is opposed to my design to introduce any discussion. The Afro-American press with one voice speaks but of unsurpassed valor, endurance, and heroism.

The National Baptist Convention attended by 5,000 delegates, representing more than 3,000,000 communicants, was held at Norfolk, Va., September 10-15.

The Herald (Austin, Texas), September 27, speaks thus of the President's annual address:

". . . President E. P. Jones' annual address was the keynote for the occasion and he sent home blow after blow, each shot followed by a bell-ring. The Convention was with him from beginning to the end. When he walked into the 'Truculent, Pussyfooting Leaders,' he had to stop until the roar of the mighty audience subsided.

"He said: 'On every gory battlefield, at every bend and turn of the road the bugle call and command were at all times obeyed and answered by your sons and the sons of those for whom you speak.

" 'They fought and died that men might be free and that the cause of liberty might walk unchallenged down the ages, unmolested and unfettered, holding high full advanced the primitive and unchangeable doctrine of: "God Our Father, Man Our Brother and Christ Our Redeemer." The World was saved from thraldrom, and through blood and fire injustice and man's inhumanity to man, let us hope, was once and for always, not only stigmatized as the galling treachery of ignorance and debauchery but condemned to despair and oblivion."

" 'Our part as American citizens in the completion of this great program must forever live and shine on down through the ages to the honor and pristine glory of those who sleep in yonder beloved land of freedom, the home of Lafayette and Clémenceau. It is hopeful when the pulpit joins and unites in demanding law and order. Every lynching is an act of barbarism, a dethronement of law and an outrage upon society. The days of its existence is short. The white man in America will yet learn that his black brother is his best friend. He died at Boston for the liberty of America, he fought from sea to sea and coast to coast to preserve the Union, and in the Argonne Forest he mixed his blood with the dust of France that the ideals of Americanism might prevail. Himself just fifty years ago a slave, he makes bare his breast to free the world and seeks only that for which the constitution has guaranteed to him.' "

The three following excerpts from editorials will indicate the character of a multitude of editorials throughout the colored press. They are representative:

"WE KNOW HOW MANY CRIMES have been committed in the name of Liberty. We condone no crimes. If a willingness to die for our liberty and our rights is a crime, then we are criminals and so was our eulogized Patrick Henry. Hark! His words: 'Give me liberty or give me death.' In the last few years we have witnessed the decadence of Negro rights, manhood rights. We have witnessed the deterioration of brotherly love. We have seen 300,000 Negroes drafted into a discriminating, segregated army and hearts of these still remain true and contrite. What a two-edged precedent. Back again to be lynched, bombed, and riot-frenzied and segregrated. WHO, THEN, SAYS THAT THE BLOOD DOES NOT CURDLE, THE TONGUE DOES NOT CLEAVE TO THE ROOF OF THE MOUTH, THE LIMBS AND EYES DULLED; WHO DOES NOT SAY: 'TAKE A MAN'S STAND?' We have no place for moral cowards. We have no place for spineless, cringing, would-be leaders who assert that this is a white man's country. Such species cannot be placed in the genus of man; men have backbone and invertebrates belong to the class reptila, example rattlesnake.

"WE WILL NOT RECRIMINATE. We who have tasted of liberty and who know that no force beneath the universe can

enslave us, have committed ourselves to the battle for liberty
and justice. The preservation of a Negro liberty under the
constitution must be a Negro's individual fight. The friends
of yester-year have been poisoned by the sinister hand of
Southern Opinion."—*The Whip* (Chicago).

"The man who can see no reason for the colored American's
unrest and dissatisfaction is either a mental misfit or totally
unacquainted with human psychology. THE BLACK MAN
FOUGHT FOR DEMOCRACY (whatever that is) and ONLY
DEMOCRACY CAN SATISFY THE INNERMOST
YEARNINGS OF HIS HEART!

"When called upon to defend his country's honor and in-
tegrity and to save civilization from the clutches of the cruel
and heartless Huns of Europe, the black American went forth
to battle the mighty Goliath of autocracy, militarism and 'kultur.' Having performed a 'brown skin' job 'over there' he
now expects Uncle Sam to clean up his own premises and
since THE BLACK MAN FOUGHT TO MAKE THE
WORLD SAFE FOR DEMOCRACY, he now demands that
AMERICA BE MADE AND MAINTAINED SAFE FOR
BLACK AMERICANS."—*The Houston Informer,* October 11.

" 'A Condition and Not a Theory Confronts Us'

Now what is the remedy in this period of reconstruction and
readjustment? It is that those who essay to lead shall redeem
their promises made to the men and women who left no stone
unturned to help save civilization. When Germany was attempting to overrun the entire civilized world to establish Prus-
sianism and tyranny, people of all races, nations and tongues
rose as one man to defeat them. They made good and Germany
was foiled in her hellish attempt. And now that they feel there
is an attempt to reëstablish the spirit of the Huns in the very
country whose chief magistrate had promised liberty and freedom to all mankind, it is most natural that they would rise up
in their might to prevent it. And this spirit of restlessness and
discontent will go on until the promise made to them on entering this war is made good. Our leaders and statesmen may as
well look facts squarely in the face: 'It is a condition that confronts us and not a theory.' They may cry peace, peace, but
there will be no peace until all classes and conditions of men

shall have equal opportunities in the race for life, liberty and the pursuit of happiness. The authorities must not make promises alone, but must fulfill them.

The people are not in the mood to submit to discrimination, or permit one class to enjoy rights and privileges at the expense of the other. They are determined to demand all the rights and privileges that are enjoyed by other classes. This was the issue that brought on the world war, and when the war was concluded, they had hoped that discrimination was at an end; but they reckoned without their host—they awoke to find that the old spirit of oppression and discrimination was still in vogue."—*The Atlanta Independent,* October 18.

2. *Discriminations Against Colored Service Men*

It may be recalled that a certain representative in Congress from South Carolina quoted from an editorial in the May number of *The Crisis,* entitled "Returning Soldiers," for the purpose of denunciation. I take another on the same subject from *The Charleston* (S. C.) *Messenger,* October 18. An attentive reading of the two will reveal a difference of rhetoric only, not of intention and substance.

"Returning Soldiers

We are returning from war. *The Crisis* and tens of thousands of black men were drafted into a great struggle. For bleeding France and what she means and has meant and will mean to us and humanity and against the threat of German race arrogance, we fought gladly and to the last drop of blood; for America and her highest ideals, we fought in far-off hope; for the dominant southern oligarchy entrenched in Washington, we fought in bitter resignation. For the America that represents and gloats in lynching, disfranchisement, caste, brutality and devilish insult—for this, in the hateful upturning and mixing of things, we were forced by vindictive fate to fight, also.

"But to-day we return! We return from the slavery of uniform which the world's madness demanded us to don to the freedom of civil garb. We stand again to look America squarely in the face and call a spade a spade. We sing: This country of ours, despite all its better souls have done and dreamed, is yet a shameful land.

"It *lynches*.

"And lynching is barbarism of a degree of contemptible nastiness unparalleled in human history. Yet for fifty years we have lynched two Negroes a week, and we have kept this up right through the war.

"It *disfranchises* its own citizens.

"Disfranchisement is the deliberate theft and robbery of the only protection of poor against rich and black against white. The land that disfranchises its citizens and calls itself a democracy lies and knows it lies.

"It encourages *ignorance*.

"It has never really tried to educate the Negro. A dominant minority does not want Negroes educated. It wants servants, dogs, whores and monkeys. And when this land allows a reactionary group by its stolen political power to force as many black folk into these categories as it possibly can, it cries in contemptible hypocrisy: 'They threaten us with degeneracy; they cannot be educated.'

"It *steals* from us.

"It organizes industry to cheat us. It cheats us out of our land; it cheats us out of our labor. It confiscates our savings. It reduces our wages. It raises our rent. It steals our profit. It taxes us without representation. It keeps us consistently and universally poor, and then feeds us on charity and derides our poverty.

"It *insults* us.

"It has organized a nation-wide and latterly a world-wide propaganda of deliberate and continuous insult and defamation of black blood wherever found. It decrees that it shall not be possible in travel nor residence, work nor play, education nor instruction for a black man to exist without tacit or open acknowledgment of his inferiority to the dirtiest white dog. And it looks upon any attempt to question or even discuss this dogma as arrogance, unwarranted assumption and treason.

"This is the country to which we Soldiers of Democracy return. This is the fatherland for which we fought! But it is *our* fatherland. It was right for us to fight. The faults of *our* country are *our* faults. Under similar circumstances, we would fight again. But by the God of Heaven, we are cowards and jackasses if now that that war is over, we do not marshal every ounce of our brain and brawn to fight a sterner, longer, more unbending battle against the forces of hell in our own land.

"We *return.*

"We *return from fighting.*

"We *return fighting.*

"Make way for Democracy! We saved it in France, and by the Great Jehovah, we will save it in the United States of America, or know the reason why."—*The Crisis.*

"Our Returned Negro Soldiers

It is such a pity that we have to put the word 'Negro' before soldiers. But, seeing we are in a country that puts a premium on the color of a person's skin instead of his or her worth, we must be content with present conditions.

"While he was away, in common with people of the other race, those of us who were left behind economized and stinted ourselves that our black boys might be as comfortable as the circumstances of war would permit.

"They did their duty at home and abroad, and now they have returned. To what have they come? Did they find a grateful country? How were they treated while in foreign lands? Let some returned Negro soldier tell the tale. We have spoken to those who have been overseas, and who only got as far as training camps. Have spoken to commissioned, 'non-coms,' as well as privates. Let them speak for themselves.

"Perhaps there might have been some officers and privates who were able to 'pass' who did not feel the curse of America's hobby. The others felt the full weight upon their defenseless heads. However, they are back from the field of carnage. Instead of the expected 'well done' they confidently and rightfully expected, what greeted them on every side? Let them tell. On every side he is met with the statement, 'niggers, as you were.'

"What does that mean? Any one familiar with conditions in America knows that meant that those soldier boys who fought as bravely as the bravest were to be lynched for the least offense, deprived of civil rights, insulted on the streets, simply because they were helpless; made to ride in filthy railroad cars; compelled to live in unsanitary sections of cities.

"There is scarcely a day that passes that newspapers don't

tell about a Negro soldier lynched in his uniform. Why do they lynch Negroes, anyhow? Have they not all the machinery of the law in their hands? With a white judge, a white jury, white public sentiment, white officers of the law, it is just as impossible for a Negro accused of crime, or even suspected of crime, to escape the white man's vengeance or his justice as it would be for a fawn to escape that wanders accidentally into a den of hungry lions. So why not give him the semblance of a trial?

"Instead of race prejudice being modified, as some of us fondly hoped, it has become intensified. The riot that started in Washington started by attacks on Negro soldiers, and from them it was only a step to killing innocent, defenseless Negroes. No one condemns a criminal Negro any sooner than we do, but we are not prepared to say that all Negroes are criminals; nor do we believe that all the criminals are Negroes. Most of the criminals caught and lynched or punished are Negroes, we will admit, but is not something wrong in that respect?

"The returned Negro soldier, as a whole, is contented with simple justice. He feels himself a man like other men, and naturally he feels that if his country saw fit to compel him to fight for it, that country, in turn, ought to at least be grateful and give him a man's chance in the race of life.

"The relatives of returned Negro soldiers were beaten and killed on the streets of Washington, right in front of the White House, under the dome of the Capitol of the greatest Republic on earth—a Republic that went to war to beat down injustice, and make the world safe for democracy. Has the the head of the nation uttered one word of condemnation of the mob? If so, we have failed to see it."—*The Charleston Messenger.*

Many acts of discrimination against colored soldiers, both during and after the war, were denounced by the colored press. The discrimination commented upon in the following editorial paragraph from *The Savannah Journal*, October 4, particularly aggrieved the Negroes:

"The fact that no American Negro troops were entered in the great peace parade in Paris on July 14th last, comes to us as a distinct shock and as another evidence of downright Ameri-

can prejudice and cussedness, practiced and evinced throughout the length and breadth of the globe. As terrible as the
shock is to us, we have the consolation, however, to know, that
in the opinion of the world, no troops of any race did their
duty more valiantly in the fight to make the world safe for
democracy, than American Negro troops."

3. The Treaty and the League of Nations

President Wilson's utterances on the rights of racial groups,
subject peoples, and safety and freedom for all quickened the
aspirations of Afro-Americans immensely. To the Conference
at Paris they looked with ardent expectations, and made a fruit-
less effort to obtain a hearing. To the Foreign Relations Committee of the United States Senate, on August 28, three national colored organizations presented amendments to the
Treaty looking to securing racial equality and protection. The
amendment proposed by the National Equal Rights League is
representative:

Amendment to Peace Treaty—New Part Proposed

"Part XVI. 'In order to make the reign of peace universal
and lasting and to make the fruits of the war effective in the
permanent establishment of true democracy everywhere the
allied and associated powers undertake, each in its own country, to secure full and complete protection of life and liberty
to all its inhabitants, without distinction of birth, nationality,
language, race or religion, and agree that all of their citizens respectively shall be equal before the law and shall enjoy
the same civil and political rights without distinction as to
race, language or religion, and all citizens of the members of
the league who belong to racial or religious minorities differing
in race or religion from the majority of the population shall
enjoy the same treatment and security in law and in fact as
all persons of the majority race or religion.' "

Regarding President Wilson's influence the following article
from The Century News Service, widely printed in colored
papers in September, must suffice:

"WILSON'S SAYINGS TORMENT SOUTH

Blame President for Causing General Unrest in Dixie

Jackson, Miss., Sept. 12.—'Who put the devil in the Negro's head?' is the question the Jones County News, a tiny sheet published in the backwoods of Mississippi, propounded to Vardaman's Weekly, edited by ex-Senator James K. Vardaman, and issued in this city. The publications referred to share honors in displaying all items derogatory to racial advancement and are said to especially cater to the ignorant element in their respective communities. From casual observations of the articles appearing in the two sheets it seems that their distinct purpose in the journalistic world is to disturb the relationship existing between the races. A quotation from the speech President Wilson delivered to a group of prominent ministers of our Race, who held a conference with him at the White House on the evening of March 14, 1918, is prefaced by this remark:

MISSISSIPPI'S QUESTION

" 'We will not tell you our opinion, but quote you from a speech of President Woodrow Wilson to a bunch of coons who called to see him. Ask yourself the question, what are the Southern people paying for this expression of Wilson's teachings which this presidential pedagogue has inculcated in the minds of the Negroes?'

"President Wilson's speech to the delegation of ministers was as follows:

THE PRESIDENT'S SPEECH

" 'I have always known that the Negro has been unjustly and unfairly dealt with; your people have exhibited a degree of loyalty and patriotism that should command the admiration of the whole nation. In the present conflict your Race has rallied to the nation's call, and if there has been any evidence of slackerism manifested by Negroes the same has not reached Washington.

" 'Great principles of righteousness are won by hard fighting and they are attained by slow degrees. With thousands of your sons in the camps and in France out of this conflict you must expect nothing less than the enjoyment of full citizenship rights —the same as are enjoyed by every other citizen.'

GIVES WARNING

"The Jones County News warns its readers in this manner:
" 'You had better quit acting the fool and stop living in the clouds and come back to the rational, sensible things on earth. Now, if you are a worshiper of Wilson, do not stop and make faces and talk about misrepresenting our President, ask yourself the above question.' "

4. *The Afro-American Tercentenary*

The Tercentenary of the importation of the Negro to the American Colonies was commemorated in all parts of the country, the proceedings in some instances continuing for several days. The commemorative programs emphasized the freshly awakened sense of racial unity and racial importance of the Afro-Americans. The addresses and papers dealt with all the phases of Negro progress and achievement, and with the problems now confronting the race. The note of grievance combined in all with the note of pride.

I will give space to two brief utterances only.

"Three Hundred Years

(TERCENTENARY, AUGUST, 1619-1919.)

Three hundred years! Lord, these are they,—
These toil-worn souls brief-sweet with play,—
    These dream-charmed people, vision-eyed,
    Whose life-free goal is yet denied.
But these have heard the heavens say,
In answer to the prayer they pray,
'No Christly cause can perish—nay,
    Though men be martyred, crucified—
Three hundred years!' "

—*Lucian B. Watkins.*

"Three Hundred Years

Three hundred years ago this month a 'Dutch man of Warre sold us twenty Negars.' They were not slaves. They were stolen freemen. They were free in Africa; they were free by the laws of Virginia. By force and fraud they and their children were gradually reduced to a slavery, the legality of which was not fully recognized for nearly a century after 1619. From their loins and the bodies of their fellows of after-years have sprung—counting both 'white' and 'black' —full twenty million souls. Those still visibly tinged with their blood are still enslaved—by compulsory ignorance, disfranchisement and public insult. In sack-cloth and ashes, then, we commemorate this day, lest we forget; lest a single drop of blood, a single moan of pain, a single bead of sweat, in all these three, long, endless centuries should drop into oblivion.

"Why must we remember? Is this but a counsel of Vengeance and Hate? God forbid! We must remember because if once the world forgets evil, evil is reborn; because if the suffering of the American Negro is once forgotten, then there is no guerdon, down to the last pulse of time, that Devils will not again enslave and maim and murder and oppress the weak and unfortunate.

"Behold, then, this month of mighty memories; celebrate it, Children of the Sun, in solemn song and silent march and grim thanksgiving. The Fourth Century dawns and through it, God guide our thrilling hands."—*The Crisis* (New York), August.

The following editorial will further emphasize the new solidarity of the Afro-Americans and their consequent greater importance:

"The United Negro

From within the Negro race there is no more hopeful sign to-day than the evidence to be seen on every hand that our people are becoming united. There is a feeling of common needs, perils, ambitions and sufferings. We think in terms of race and plan for the benefit of all. Every man speaks for his brethren. On the great questions of civil rights, social justice, political activity and industrial equality the Negro race is more nearly united than ever before.

The Negro's Reaction to the World War 43

"The race is united in sympathy for all its members who suffer wrong or injustice in any part of the country. The sentiment is growing that an injury to one is an injury to all.
An insult to one on account of color is an insult intended to
humiliate all. Discrimination against the individual Negro is
for the purpose of putting a bar before the whole race. Every
member of the race becomes its representative. Legislation
that seeks to restrict the rights of the race unites the race in
a common struggle for justice. Agitators against the race drive
the members together with the impulse of mutual protection
against a common danger. Every speech against the Negro
in Congress or on the lecture platform strengthens the unity
of the race. At the beginning of the American Revolution one
of the old colonial flags had inscribed upon it the words, 'unite
or die.' The Negro is reading history and learning lessons.

"The Negro race is becoming united through great religious,
fraternal, business and professional organizations whose membership is race wide and nation wide. In the meetings held by
these different bodies Negroes come together from all parts of
the country. They are coming to know the leaders of all sections and the conditions under which our people live in the
North and South, the East and West. Gatherings of this kind
that call together thousands of our people are held every year
in some of our great cities. As these organizations grow
larger and become more representative of the entire life of
the colored people, they will tend to establish a stronger bond
of union for the entire race.

"The Negro race is united through the colored newspapers
that now have a circulation reaching every state and city where
there are large numbers of our people. In the general welfare
of the race, in its progress and advancement, in efforts for
education, in the promotion of business and in all matters that
pertain to our peculiar trials and difficulties the Negro press
presents a united front for the good of all of our people. The
Negro race is united in harmony of thought in regard to its
rights as citizens in this country. These thoughts may find
expression in many different and seemingly discordant expressions, but in the great fundamental things that are essential for human life, prosperity and happiness, the members of
our race are practically united in their feelings, desires and demands. We will always have differences in regards to plans
and methods. But with a united people so far as the great
and vital issues are concerned we shall move on toward success

twelve million strong."—*The Charleston* [S. C.] *Messenger,*
September 13.

5. *Negro Congresses*

"The Convention Season

The convention period is on and men and women are fore-
gathering to renew old friendships and discuss matters of fraternity and business, as well as plan for the future.

"This is especially true of the many conventions that are now
or are about to be held by various racial interests. The delegates represent various interests, are leaders in their respective
communities and, coming as they do from all sections of the
country, can exert a most powerful influence in behalf of the
race.

"Even though these gatherings may live up to the letter and
spirit of their chartered purposes for existing, each will fail
to do its duty that neglects to sound a warning that the professions of interest in the uplift of the status of other peoples
that this government so insistently makes will be discounted as
long as the colored citizens of this country are kept in a state
of partial subjection and denied those rights so freely accorded
other classes of citizens."—*The Afro-American* (Baltimore).

That pronouncement will serve to introduce the subject of
Negro congresses and to suggest their general purpose. There
have been several congresses, national in representation, held
during the summer, each with a specific purpose, but all em-
phasizing the problems of reconstruction for the Negro and
all directing their chief attention to the grievances of their
people and measures for remedy.

A forerunner to the National race congresses of the summer was the Pan-African Congress held in Paris in February.
The Afro-American situation was there brought, as it were,
into an international court. *The Odd Fellows Journal* (Washington, D. C.), July 3, contained a two-column report of this
congress, copied from *The Peace Advocate.* This congress was
significant as a manifestation of that movement toward unity
of feeling, interest, and action which is prevalent throughout

the branches of the African people, all of which, apparently, were represented.

Afro-French utterances contrasted French and American treatment of the Negro. In another section evidence will be found that French doctrine and example have been potent in prompting Afro-Americans to the demands they are now putting forward. The utterances of the Afro-Americans in this congress were bitterly denunciatory of their country, according to the article alluded to.

A few of the more significant national race congresses of the summer will here be given space in the order of their occurrence. The annual convention of The National Association for the Advancement of the Colored People was held in Cleveland in July, and was attended by 265 delegates from thirty-four states. Addresses were made in accordance with the purposes of this organization and the newly kindled feelings of the colored people and their friends. The objects of this association are set forth as follows:

"NATIONAL ASSOCIATION

FOR THE

ADVANCEMENT OF COLORED PEOPLE

Organized, February, 1909

Incorporated, May, 1911

"1. To abolish legal injustice against Negroes.

"2. To stamp out race discriminations.

"3. To prevent lynchings, burnings and torturings of black people.

"4. To assure to every citizen of color the common rights of American citizenship.

> *President Wilson declared for woman suffrage as a war measure. Black men are not allowed to vote in many of the states of the Union, despite the Fifteenth Amendment.*

"5. To compel equal accommodations in railroad travel, irrespective of color.

"6. To secure for colored children an equal opportunity to

public school education through a fair apportionment of public education funds. *Unless the colored child can be educated he is at a fearful disadvantage. An uneducated Negro population menaces national well-being. This education should be of hand and brain and can be adequately done* for all Negro children, not the fortunate few, *only by public schools.*

"7. To emancipate in fact, as well as in name, a race of nearly 12,000,000 American-born citizens.

"The only means we can employ are education, organization, agitation, publicity—the force of an enlightened public opinion. "THE WORK IS SUPPORTED ENTIRELY BY VOLUNTARY CONTRIBUTIONS AND MEMBERSHIPS."

The Crisis is the official organ of the Association. It has a circulation of more than 100,000 copies.

In the latter part of September the National Equal Rights League held its twelfth annual session in the city of Washington.

The following extracts from what seems to have been the most notable address, it alone being printed in full in *The Guardian*, October 4, doubtless represent the general thought and temper of the Equal Rights League:

FORK OF THE ROADS

"In our racial life and activities we have reached the fork of the roads. One goes straight ahead—one turns to the left and one to the right. Which shall we take?

"The road along which we have been traveling is well known to us. It has given us property and education—property which has been taxed while representation has been denied us—education which has been placed at the service of the State, which has disfranchised and segregated us and subjected the race to all manner of villainies which have increased and not decreased while we have been traveling forward in the development of our material and educational opportunities.

"The road turning to the left is the road of supine submission to every illegal and criminal villainy, and those who would guide us down this road will betray us into the hands of our enemies in exchange for place and gold.

"The road turning to the right is full of hardship and danger, but in all stages of the world those who have taken it and stood its tests have come into possession of the promised land of LIBERTY and EQUALITY.

.   .   .   .

"To-day, men everywhere throughout the world are clamoring for democratic governments—for equal civil and political rights and the abolition of special privileges.

"The man of Europe has been remade along these lines since the November armistice—and the men 'farthest down' have entirely disappeared from Europe, where thrones and privileged classes have been thrown into the dust heaps of popular wrath.

"Shall we colored men then—here in this country for which our fathers fought in every war which has swept across its bosom be satisfied with anything less than our guaranteed constitutional liberties?

"Shall we struggle in an organized and intelligent manner for these rights and liberties, or shall we leave an inheritance of shame and dishonor to our children—weigh them down with responsibilities which we must now assume, if we are men?

RIGHTS ARE DENIED

"In twelve Southern States our people are denied the right to vote—compelled to ride in 'Jim Crow' cars—denied the right to enter public libraries, denied the right to serve on juries, denied the right to occupy a seat in a public park, their lives are taken by mobs, the members of which go unwhipped of justice; our women are prostituted by lecherous white beasts who are protected by the absence of a bastardy law, and by another law which makes intermarriage a criminal offense.

"These and many other barbarous indignities are put upon us, and the time has now come when in the great work of national reconstruction this organization must gird up its loins, put on its armor and prepare to fight with every legal weapon allowed this diabolical American spirit, which has brought upon and inflicted us with these evils."

The National Race Congress followed in the second week of October in Washington. On the subject of congresses, apropos of this one, I quote from *The Washington Eagle* an article accredited to *The Indianapolis Freeman*:

"RACE CONGRESS FORTUNATE IN LEADERSHIP

Unqualified Endorsement of Foremost Race Protective Organization by a Standard Negro Journal

The Indianapolis Freeman, one of the ablest exponents of Negro thought and progressive race activity in this country, in a recent editorial thus 'struck the nail on the head' in its comment on the suffrage session of the National Race Congress of America, which is to meet in Washington next Tuesday:

A PEOPLE OFTTIMES MUST CREATE A CONGRESS OF ITS OWN

" 'A people who have no direct representation in the national legislature must ofttimes make a congress of their own, in order to give adequate and timely consideration to the many questions that affect their daily life and well-being. This is the situation in which the Negro people of this country find themselves to-day. It is this situation that has made the formation of the National Race Congress an urgent necessity. Appropriately, it assembles in Washington, the seat of the National Government, where 'it may come closely into contact with and more intimately impress the members of the authorized lawmaking body of the republic. If it can not make laws, it can make sentiment, which is more powerful than laws and which is ever the forerunner to all reforms. * * * The predominance of the ballot in the working out of the race's salvation is so apparent that the promoters of the movement have felt justified in styling the meeting of October 7 a "suffrage session." * * * The colored people everywhere recognize the critical conditions that are confronting us and realize that only by prompt and vigorous action all along the line may we hope to enjoy the rights and privileges vouchsafed us by the Constitution and the laws. The propaganda of those who would despoil us of our birthright of citizenship is spread constantly and universally—openly, where it is possible to be open—and with a subtlety that almost defies detection, where secrecy and indirection are regarded as necessary to the accomplishment of their devilish purposes. This propaganda must be met and defeated. To protect the welfare of the Negro millions in this country is the mission the National Race Congress has taken upon itself, and right royally has it labored toward this end during the three years of its existence. * * * It is the best known and most generally accepted Negro protective organization in the land.' "

A very full report of the proceedings of this Congress appeared in many papers, too full to be quoted here. *The Afro-American* (Baltimore), October 10, contained the following abridgement:

"FOURTH ANNUAL SESSION OF NATIONAL BODY STARTS MONDAY

Thousands Attend

Washington, October 9.—Definite plans for making democracy safe for the Negro, race discriminations, lynchings and the establishment of a bureau for the spreading of accurate information about the Negro, were among the things discussed at the fourth annual session of the National Race Congress, which has been meeting at Metropolitan Baptist Church since Monday.

"The Congress is being attended by representative men and women from all parts of the country. Those from the South, where discriminations are most galling, are strongly urging that efforts must be made to remedy anti-racial conditions. A number of Marylanders are among those in attendance. The sessions will continue through Saturday.

"In his annual address, President William H. Jernagin said: 'To-day, by the action of a dominant political group from Maryland to Texas, your people and my people are herded together and separated from other people with a stamp of inferiority and difference as travelers in every kind of public tramway and mode of communication. To-day, your people and my people are intimidated and legislated from the free exercise of the right of suffrage and its concomitant in a republican form of government: the right to hold and administer public office, if they happen to live in those States where their prepondering numbers and its result in contribution to the material wealth of the commonwealth, entitles them to such franchise and such office.'

"Rev. F. J. Goodall, of Savannah, Ga., asserted that the leaders among the race must get hold of the common people and lead them in the fight for equal rights.

"Bishop George W. Clinton declared 'that there can be no right adjustment until the white and colored people share the same privileges.'"

This Congress's "Address to the Country" was to the same general effect as this editorial. Each of these congresses with their speeches and resolutions and appeals occupied much space in the colored papers throughout the summer and fall. They attest one supreme interest in the colored people.

IV. THE NEGRO'S GRIEVANCES AND DEMANDS

"WHAT the Negro wants with all his heart, and what America will proudly concede him, I do believe, can be stated very easily.

" 'In substitution for lynchings, he wants justice in the courts; he wants the privilege of serving on juries; the right to vote; the right to hold office like other citizens. He wants better educational facilities; abolition of the "Jim Crow" car and of discrimination and segregation in the Government service; the same military training and chance for promotion in the army that white men enjoy; destruction of the peonage system, an equal wage, better housing, better sanitary conditions and reforms in Southern penal institutions.

" 'That is the Negro problem. Does it impose too much upon the greatest democracy in the world? I cannot believe that it does.' "—Dr. Emmet J. Scott, Secretary-Treasurer of Howard University, in *The Atlanta Post*.

The grievances and demands of the Negro are expressed through all his channels of publicity—speeches, addresses, sermons, petitions, resolutions, news reports, stories, poems, editorials. Of all these his weekly paper is the clearing-house.

From an unlimited accumulation of protesting, appealing, menacing, indignant, resolute utterances, I have selected what appeared to be the most typical and comprehensive. Against every form and kind of discrimination, exclusion and proscription on account of color the Negro press is almost universally uttering its protest, now mild, now angry, but always firm. His reasons, too, are set forth and his cause is urged home by every kind of device and discourse known to reformers.

KNOWING THE NEGRO

"What the white man does not know and what real Negro leaders need to truthfully and fearlessly tell him, is just

51

exactly what the Negro does want. Such procedure would go far toward bringing about the much desired better understanding and the lead to such adjustment as would be of benefit to both races. When the white man knows that the Negro is dissatisfied and knows not what would satisfy him, he is in a suspicious frame of mind; but to know what is really in the Negro's mind, puts him at ease and in position to adjust matters on the most satisfactory basis. Our white friends would regard our leaders more highly if they would candidly express true race sentiment. The Negro is satisfied to confine social aspirations within his own race: but he does want such political and economic rights as are guaranteed to every law-abiding citizen under the constitution of our country.

"The Negro wants the right to earn a decent livelihood; to accumulate property according to his ability and to have his property rights protected. The Negro wants better school facilities; a chance to educate his children; justice in the courts and executions by law instead of by lynchers. We believe that the fair-minded element of white people are willing that the Negro should have these things and that with the friendly coöperation of the responsible classes within both races in seeking to bring about such conditions, race friction would be at a minimum; there would be no need for the Negro to seek better conditions elsewhere and that the Southern Negro and the Southern white man would be able to dwell together in peace and in the spirit of mutual helpfulness."—*The Hot Springs* [Ark.] *Echo*, September 20.

"A Potent Factor In Race Disturbances

The Federal Government, the management of political parties, the Church of Jesus Christ and all other public institutions which proclaim democracy and the Fatherhood of God and the Brotherhood of Man and yet persist in ignoring the colored man's right to representation are potent factors in aiding and abetting the spirit of disturbance and mob law which is abroad in the land. When a government calls a labor congress and refuses representation to the colored race, which forms a large proportion of the labor element—when a political party calls a conference for party success and ignores an important element in the success of that party—when a church refuses to accord to a race the right of its own leadership in its highest ecclesiastical councils—when judiciaries refuse to put him on juries where the interest of his own race is involved, and when, too, all this is done because of his race and color, then the institutions so acting only proclaim their cherished but mistaken belief in the inferiority of the race, which attitude on their part simply serves as a stimulus for the lawless element to prey upon the unfortunate members of that race for every and any kind of offense, real and imaginary. This is not true only in the case of colored people, but it is true anywhere there is a minority element and treated in like manner. The majority or dominant element proceeds on the assumption that the colored man is inferior; that he is not his so-called social equal, and that therefore it can treat him according to its own notion and with impunity, since the judges, policemen and all the elements which compose these institutions are white men.

"Of course, in the majority of cases, this lawless crowd has often received a set back, but it is nevertheless true that this is the principle upon which they proceed. Let these institutions referred to in the foregoing and all others of which the colored man is a factor, recognize the principles of democracy, for which he died in France as bravely and as heroically as the white man, and the land will enjoy peace and prosperity."— *The Commonwealth* (Baltimore), October 10.

The following editorial in *The Cleveland Advocate* of October 18 was extensively copied:

"President Wilson's Illness

. . . .

There is nothing vindictive in the Colored American. His years of oppression have brought home to him, perhaps more forcibly than to any other class, the trite expression, 'Sorrow makes the whole world kin.'

"It requires no stretch of imagination to remind the 12,000,-000 Colored people of these United States that race prejudice has obtained to a far greater degree under the present national Democratic administration than at any time since the close of the War of the Rebellion.

. . . .

"But now there is a universal plea for prayer for his recovery and we, too, must join in the general supplication. Therefore, let us pray.

"Let us pray, forsooth, let us pray that:

"President Wilson will fully recover;

"That we will be given the courage to speak out against the wrongs of humanity at home;

"That Congress will get the nerve to enforce the Constitution or cut representation;

"That national law-makers will not be permitted to defy the law in the face of the public and go unchallenged or unpunished;

"That the Railroad Administration will not tolerate American citizens riding in cars of dilapidation and filth;

"That universal and compulsory education may drive out the demon of ignorance;

"That courts of real justice may take the place of the gun, the torch, and the rope;

"That honor and respect be accorded ALL women, with emphasis on the 'all';

"That industrial opportunity everywhere be based strictly on merit and worth;

"That petty politics and professional political bargaining may be relegated to the deserved oblivion;

"That the Associated Press, and any similar organization of newspapers, will discontinue coloring up their news where our group is affected;

"That the terms—Democracy, Liberty, Freedom, Justice, Opportunity, and Manhood Rights—will mean what they seem to mean, and have the same meaning in our country as they do abroad. 'LET US PRAY.'"

The Chicago Whip, August 9, affords a summary that must here conclude a subject on which the colored editors have written and are still writing so much:

"The High Cost of Being a Negro

In the textile industries in New England, salaries have increased 60 per cent while the salaries of Negroes who make their jobs a possibility are only raised 25 per cent. White men doing the same work are getting twice the amount in salaries. The articles manufactured are put upon the market and the negro has to pay the same price for them as the whites who are getting better wages.

"IN CHICAGO, KANSAS CITY, NEW YORK AND DE-
TROIT WHERE NEGROES ARE WORKING, GETTING
THE SAME SALARIES AS THE WHITES, THEY HAVE
TO PAY TWICE THE RENT, AND IN NEIGHBORHOOD
CLOTHING AND GROCERY STORES, RECENT INVES-
TIGATIONS SHOW THAT FOR THE SAME GRADE OF
GOODS, THE NEGRO HAS TO PAY, BESIDES THE
RAISE THAT IS SUPPOSED TO BE JUSTIFIED BY
THE GENERAL CHANGE IN ECONOMIC CONDITIONS,
AN ADDITIONAL COLOR TAX, SOMETIMES AS HIGH
AS 50 PER CENT; THUS HIS NET EARNINGS, IF ANY
AT ALL, ARE 50 PER CENT LESS THAN THE WHITE
WORKERS.   BY PERVERTED SOCIAL CONVENTION,
BOMBS AND RIOTS, HE IS FORCED INTO A CERTAIN
TERRITORY WHERE HE IS BLACKJACKED OUT OF
HIS EARNINGS.

"Very recently in some of the larger cities, anti-negro propaganda has been spread by scheming criminal and low white
real estate men for their personal gain.   In such districts, white
business men have been threatened with boycott if they did not
discharge colored help.   Several hundred colored people have
been thrown out of profitable employment on this account.   Just
because they were negroes. The sequence is that the whole race
has an additional expense.   In the political world, which to a
great extent overlaps the industrial and economic, his status
is the same.   It costs him to be a negro.   In the Second Ward
alone, where he constitutes 85 per cent of the majority of the
population, he only gets 15 per cent of the patronage, including
the civil service.   Therefore, he is robbed of the difference between the 15 and 85.

"If all of the data relative to the additional expense and dis-
advantages that are singular to the negro besides the general
disadvantage all have to suffer, a brain devoid of anything but
density could easily perceive why the high cost of living as it
affects the general public pales into insignificance in comparison
with the high cost of being a negro.   IN FACT, THE COL-
ORED MAN HAS SO MUCH TOLERANCE AND ENDUR-
ANCE ABOVE THAT OF THE OTHER GROUPS, THERE
ARE VERY SERIOUS DOUBTS IF HE WOULD KICK
AT ALL IF HE WAS ONLY AFFECTED AS THE RE-
MAINDER OF THE POPULATION.   The high cost of being
a negro is one of the most pathetic incidents in the universe to-
day and along the lines of general democracy unless the cost

is lessened 'the heart of the world will be broken' and especially
the negro's own heart because 'he is on the operating table, but
without an anesthetic.' (Aid the Belgian relief and feed starv-
ing France.)"

A few of the specific fundamental demands of the colored
race will here be given each a separate section.

1. *The Ballot*

In the call for the fourth annual session of the National
Race Congress, which was to be a suffrage session, was this
paragraph:

"The right to vote and to be voted for, is the first of rights,"
says the National Race Congress. "It is the vital principle of
self-government and individual liberty. The ballot marks the
difference between the citizen and the serf. Without the ballot
the colored American is powerless to contend for right and
justice and civil equality; with the ballot he is all-powerful to
act in defense of every lawful privilege."

That seems to put in a nutshell the Negro's doctrine of the
ballot.

The colored papers in every part of the country strongly appeal to their people to register and vote, particularly on local
issues. "The right to vote and to be voted for" is a slogan.
The Afro-American (Baltimore), October 10, affords a representative utterance, which I take from one of many editorial
appeals:

"There is no class of citizenry that should value the right to
vote more than the colored people. Wrongs are to be righted,
privileges are to be secured and the ballot is the most effective
weapon to be used for accomplishing beneficial results."

The same paper, October 24, addressed to all the state
candidates in Maryland these questions which were extensively
copied throughout the land:

"BALTIMORE'S METHOD OF HAND-LING OFFICE SEEKERS

Significant Questionnaire Contains Suggestions for Voters

BALTIMORE, Oct. 23.—The Afro-American, one of the most aggressive newspapers of the country, is sending out questionnaires as to all candidates' stand on various questions. A sample of the questionnaire follows:

"If elected to the office to which you aspire, would you use your best efforts:

"1. To secure equal appropriations for teachers' salaries and school accommodations throughout the state of Maryland? Answer yes or no.

"2. To see that all citizens of the state have equally long school terms? Answer yes or no.

"3. To see that the compulsory school attendance law be rigidly enforced throughout the state? Answer yes or no.

"4. To see that the legislature take the necessary steps to nullify the Jim Crow car law throughout the state? Answer yes or no.

"5. To see that the legislature appropriate a sum of not less than $35,000 a year for Victory hospital, a non-sectarian institution located in Baltimore city, which is to be used as the state hospital for colored people? Answer yes or no.

"6. To see that wherever a case in any court in the state involves either a colored plaintiff or defendant one or more members of the jury will also be colored? Answer yes or no.

"7. To clean up the gambling and disorderly houses, which are being run by persons for white and colored patrons? Answer yes or no."

From *The Guardian* (Boston), July 12, I take these statements:

"Three-fourths of the Negroes of the United States, who own more than seven hundred million dollars worth of property are deprived of the right to vote. A white man's vote in Mississippi amounts to 13 votes in Kansas. A white man's vote in Alabama is equivalent to 11 votes in Minnesota. The comparison is quite similar in any southern state."

The two following editorial appeals from the same issue of the same paper are representative of the present activity of the colored press in the matter of voting:

"Thanks to our committee on registration, our Negro men are beginning to awaken themselves to this particular duty of citizenship—They are beginning to realize what it means to them as individuals and to the race to become registered voters. This action on their part is a good sign of the times and augurs well the coming of the day when our men will be men in every sense of the word. May the good work of the committee continue until every Negro man of the voting age of Savannah and Chatham county becomes a registered voter." —*The Savannah Journal,* November 1.

In another column in the course of a featured appeal to register and vote, was this exhortation:

. . . .

"Let us continue actively in the matter of registration. It is necessary that in a city of 45,000 colored people, 10,000 of them should pay taxes and register. The ballot is the weapon of a peaceful war. In the war of peace, no man is armed without it. A man without a vote in peace time is as powerless as a man without a gun in war time. No government, municipal, state nor national, heeds the demands of a voteless race."

2. Participation in Government

The Negro bases his demand for the ballot upon his constitutional rights and his demand for participation in government upon the principles of Anglo-Saxon civilization. More specifically, he is a citizen and claims his rights under the constitution, putting forward as reinforcements to his demands the educational fitness of his race, its vital interests as a large property owner, and its services to the country in peace and in war.

Specific demands pertaining to local government are numerous in every part of the country: representation on school-boards, in city councils, in the police force, on the boards of public institutions of all kinds; also in the administration of justice and in the making of laws. The slogan of the Colonists in '76 the Negro has made his own to-day:

"Taxation Without——

'Taxation without representation' is the slogan that fired the souls of the American Revolutionists, brought about that memorable social event, 'The Boston Tea Party,' and furnished the means by which Crispus Attucks, Negro, was the first to shed his blood for American Liberty and Independence.

"Twelve million of Attucks' kindred now form one-tenth of the population of our great nation, a number more than three times the population of the Thirteen Original States in those days. There is a group in this nation that insists on depriving the people of the Negro Race from voting, and yet, in the matter of taxation, the Negro is required to pay. The Negro is counted in making up representation for Congress, but he is not allowed to become part of it; he is counted in selecting soldiers to defend the Union, but he is denied the right to say who shall govern him.

"Those who deny furnish neither alibi nor apology. They do not claim it to be either righteous or just, they simply say it is expedient. They protest for Ireland, and Poland and Slavs and what nots, and keep the hand of oppression upon us. They are determined that this method shall continue, world without end. They claim it is the only 'safe way for the 'superior race' to keep the 'inferior race' down.' They regard the Constitution of the United States, if not as a mere scrap of paper, certainly an untimely document. Their conscience, like a false face, is put on and taken off at will. They say their way MUST continue. We say, GOD IS JUST."—*The Houston Informer.*

The Houston Observer, October 25, sets forth in the following editorial, one of many such at hand, why the Negro should have part in all the business of government:

"Where Interest Is Centered

There is a deal of speculation among colored citizens as to the disposition of the school authorities after the school tax election. If the election carries, which seems reasonably certain, just how much of a spirit of fairness will be shown the colored teacher by the School Board? Of course there will be an increase; no one doubts that very much, but no one has forgotten that 'measly' increase of 25 cents per day given the colored teachers last June. Unnecessary to mention what other teachers received at that time, and any way, it is sacrilege in the South to make comparisons of the kind.

"But, in the name of common sense, truth and justice, when is the South going to outgrow that despicable and hated custom of imposing on, riding on, saving on and 'getting by' on Negro wage earners? It is, and has long been nauseating to the Negro people to meet such constant, unrelenting and inconsistent discrimination at every turn and at all times. It would discourage and sour any other people.

"For a century this country has harbored and nurtured foreign peoples from nearly all parts of the world. All doors are flung wide for them; their children educated; recreation and comforts are furnished them in an effort to make them at home, just to have lots of them return to their native lands when 'fattened', taking wealth with them. All this—while the black boy and girl, whose parents and grand-parents made the South rich, are kept as close to those slavery days as this government will permit.

"It is that old spirit of slavery, i. e., that there must be no equality between master and servant, that is heaping so many injustices on the struggling Negro race. It is this same spirit that the colored voters and tax-payers, who pay an equal rate of taxation, are watching in the School Board. They are for the tax and anything else that means advancement; but they are honestly tired of that old traditional southern policy. They know that the machinery of this modern age is not operated on tradition, but on actual cash or its economic equivalent. Some of the more spirited of them would force an issue on this question if any good could derive therefrom. Who can blame them?"

An example of good counsel given by a Negro editor and accepted by the white authorities is afforded by *The Houston Informer,* October 11, which relates how a colored patrolman, appointed at this paper's suggestion "cleared up Milam."

Coöperation between the two races would seem to be a reasonable desire. All the colored papers are constantly urging it,—coöperation in the making of law, in the administration of law, in the maintenance of law and order. In regard to voluntary coöperation, or "getting together," this the last part of an editorial in *The Atlanta Independent,* October 25, is representative:

"We are informed that from time to time the black and white preachers meet together and discuss matters. Whether these matters are for the benefit and edification of those who discuss them or for the benefit of the public, one can hardly judge from the fruits they bear. However, we will grant the movement the charity to believe it was organized in good faith, and its actions, if it has any, make for the uplift of the community.

"There are thousands of things this alliance could do if they are going to make Christ a factor in the community life. It could denounce lynch law, bolshevism, Jim Crow cars, Jim Crow elevators and contend for every citizen to enjoy equal privileges and benefits before the law. The white-black preachers' alliance or coöperative movement could protest against double sessions in Negro schools, against insufficient pay for Negro teachers, against dilapidated, broken down school houses for Negro children—against unsanitary and unhealthful conditions in Negro schools. It could plead with the authorities of the office buildings in the city to allow the Negroes more than one elevator in office buildings, and protest against white people crowding the Negroes off the one elevator allowed for them— boxes, plunder and freight. They could sound the gospel trumpet from the pulpit every Sunday against the mobs and mob law, which is sweeping this entire country. It could demand better streets in Negro communities and better fire and police protection. It could at least ask the city authorities to sweep the streets sometimes in communities where Negroes live. On Auburn avenue, where the Negroes have quite a million dollars invested, the streets are never swept—neglected simply because Negroes own the property."

3. *The Administration of Justice*

The discriminations against colored people in regard to arrest, imprisonment, trial and punishment weigh most heavily upon them. They complain that they are at the mercy of a brutal police, a prejudiced judge and a jury on which he is not represented. The standard of justice is one thing for the white man, another thing for the black man.

The Savannah Journal thus writes of the discrimination practiced in that city:

"Not Like Savannah

The wholesale and indiscriminate arrests of colored citizens of the city should not be countenanced by the authorities of the city. The practice is bad when it is considered that no crime has been committed.

"The arrest of our business men should be discontinued. These men are active in the effort to stamp out idleness by furnishing employment for our people. They commit no crime. Their minds have no criminal tendency. 'Uppishness' as a Negro's pride is termed, is not as yet penalized. Then we are of the opinion that the charge of 'uppishness' will not hold good in law and arrests based upon such charges should be discontinued.

"We want peace. We desire to encourage thrift. We want to see a just application of the law in cases where flagrant disregard of the law is evidenced. We believe that the law should 'command what is right and prohibit what is wrong.' But we do not believe that 'new wrongs' should be created and made applicable to the Negro alone."

From *The Mobile Forum*, October 18, I take the following:

"Negroes Do Not Condone Crime

It has been stated, especially by some of our neighbors, that Negro leaders and those who endeavor to give the Negroes a square deal in the courts and fields of labor in America so that right and justice may be his portion along with the other group of citizens do not devote enough of their time and effort in preventing crime, and this charge against the leaders and friends of our race is based on a false assumption prompted by race prejudice.

"If there is any set of people in this or any other country who think that the Negro is so instinctively criminal that it is necessary for the leaders of the race to form organizations to teach him to obey the laws of the land, they are badly mistaken.

"The leaders among the Negro race, and those who have helped our cause do not condone crimes committed by white or black, and we naturally hate to hear of a crime committed by those whom we are trying to help, but we do not see why the crime of one class should be magnified and the other class considered as a matter of course.

"All the Negro asks is a fair trial in the courts and an equal chance as a wage earner. We do not hide or attempt to hide the criminals among us. All we ask is 'equal justice before the law.'

"It was remarked in one of the courts in Georgia a few days ago that not half the colored men in U. S. who are sentenced would be convicted if they were properly represented before the courts of that state. If that is the case in Georgia it must be the same way in many other states. This accounts for the penal institutions of the land being the abiding place for so many of our race."

One of the most outspoken statements of the Negro's case I find in *The Black Dispatch* (Oklahoma City), October 10. It is a speech delivered by the editor of that paper before a meeting called by and presided over by Governor Robertson and attended by both races. The circumstances are important, for it is a good omen when a state governor takes such a step to bring about racial adjustment as was taken in this instance. Only extracts from this thoroughly representative speech can here be given:

"The cornerstone upon which rests all of our difficulties is YOUR UNWILLINGNESS TO RECOGNIZE THE NEGRO AS A MAN. Now the Negro is a man, and a free man. I might say to make clearer my point that you have now with you a NEW NEGRO. I do not mean the new Negro that you have had described to you. You have had what was termed a NEW NEGRO described to you as an insolent, arrogant individual, a creature who would not assimilate himself properly into organized forms of government. I mean this, that out of the education that you have permitted us to get and which we have acquired out of our own efforts also, there has developed a different creature than the inert clod that you once knew as a slave. IN YOUR FAILURE TO RECOGNIZE JUST THIS ONE FACT RESTS ALL OF THE DIFFICULTY.

.   .   .   .

"This New Negro, who stands to-day released in spirit, finds himself, in America and in this state, physically bound and shackled by LAWS AND CUSTOMS THAT WERE MADE FOR SLAVES, and all of the unrest, all of the turbulence and all of the violence that now is charged to my people IS THE BATTLE OF FREE MEN, POUNDING UPON WALLS THAT SURROUND THEM AND THAT WERE MADE FOR SLAVES.

.   .   .   .

"I am alarmed at the idea that some of the people of this country have as to the cause of the unrest among us. Some say, if I read correctly your newspapers, that there are I. W. W. agitators among us. Others say that it is Bolshevik or anarchistic influences that seek to draw us into their radical division. This is an improper conclusion. The Negro has arrived at the place where he now finds himself through his own processes of reasoning. For example, it does not take an I. W. W. to clinch the argument that the majority of the Negroes in the United States cannot vote. It does not take an anarchist to ride with us on the railroad for us to know that when we pay three cents per mile that we do not get what you get by paying the same and identical amount. It does not take a Bolshevist to inform us that freedom of movement is restricted to us and that, under the guise of law a separate status as citizens is designed for the black man.

"I think you ought to know how the black man talks and feels at times when he knows that you are nowhere about, and I want to tell you, if you were to creep up to-night to a place where there are 10,000 Negroes gathered, you would find no division on this one point. I know that they all would say, 'WE HAVE NO CONFIDENCE IN WHITE POLICEMEN.'

.   .   .   .

"Let there be one hundred or one hundred thousand, they would with one accord all say, WE HAVE NO CONFIDENCE IN THE WHITE MAN'S COURT. I think you ought to know this, for it is with what men think that we have to deal. They would say in such a meeting that they know before they get into the court what the verdict will be. If their cause is the cause of a black man against a white man they will say that they know that a verdict would be rendered in favor of the white man.

"Now what is the psychology in this situation? How does the black man's mind operate under such conditions? If a Negro commits an offense he is apt to think like this, 'I cannot turn myself over to the police, FOR IT IS THE MOB; neither can I afford to turn myself over to the court, for it will lynch me of justice,' and he reaches this final conclusion, that there are two avenues open to him, EITHER SUCCESSFULLY HIDE OR FIGHT AND DIE. How would you feel and how do you think that the Negro feels laboring under such conditions?

"None of my race is dreaming of what you so often term 'SOCIAL EQUALITY.'

. . . . . .

"What we want is 'SOCIAL JUSTICE.' We want to feel a larger security in our homes from the hand of the mob. We want the free, untrammeled right at the ballot box. We want justice in the courts and the right, under the law, to do anything that other citizens of this government may do."

. . . . . . |●|

4. *Social Equality*

This is the crux. Almost the first question raised regarding the colored press is, "Does it preach social equality?" An unqualified monosyllable cannot be given in answer. First, because the colored press, while generally united in its purposes and efforts, does not hold to one manner of speech on all subjects. Secondly, because the question requires interpretation. It is capable of different meanings and implications. Thirdly, the question is so dangerous in the South that the colored papers there either keep away from it or pooh-pooh the idea. A very few papers, without being specific on this question, demand "absolute equality."

Whatever variety of view and expression there may be in the colored press will be represented in the selections that follow:

"The *St. Luke Herald* [Richmond, Va.], of which Mrs. Maggie L. Walker is the managing editor, rises to remark: 'All the talk about the colored press encouraging social equality is a Southern made lie, invented and copyrighted that the South might have an excuse to justify it in the maltreatment of our race.' Mrs. Walker hit the nail on the head. Social equality 'is a homemade bugaboo,' invented by Southern demagogues for domestic consumption chiefly."—*The New York Age.*

The *Chicago Whip*, one of the new weeklies, affords the following utterances, in a long editorial, August 9:

"Has the Negro Been Fighting For Social Equality?

We have made an accurate survey of the claims of the new Negro. We have censored his activities since his return from France. And we even aided the investigators of Chicago dailies as they followed the color line. We have gathered first hand information from Washington, D. C., as to the feeling of its colored people. WE FAIL YET TO OBSERVE WHERE THE NEGRO HAS MADE ANY FIGHT FOR SOCIAL EQUALITY. . . . Yet they claim the Negro is fighting for social equality when he buys property in sections where before he was a stranger. THEY CALL THIS AN INVASION.

"We admit that the Negro is tired of being a 'half-man.' We admit that he is tired of the heel of white oppression. We admit that he has been pushed to the wall and even he now stands and shows his teeth. We even admit that the Negro desires social EQUALITY ON THE BASIS OF MERIT. BUT WE CANNOT BE INTELLIGENTLY HONEST AND TRUTHFULLY ADMIT THAT HE HAS MADE ANY FIGHT FOR SOCIAL EQUALITY. HIS FIGHT HAS BEEN A DEFENSIVE ONE. THIS SEEMS SURPRISING AND ALARMING TO OUR WHITE FRIENDS, WHO SEEM TO THINK THAT HE SHOULD BE PASSIVELY SUBMISSIVE.

"WE KNOW HOW American soldiers and sailors infested France with their damnable prejudice. We know that the Negro's soul has rankled with hate and resentment. We also know that white soldiers and marines led the mobs in Washington. Lest we forget, the mobs in the loop were commandeered by sailors and soldiers.

"Did it ever occur to you that our white friends really fear that the Negro is breaking his shell and beginning to bask in the sunlight of real manhood? "IS IT THE DESIRE OF THE WHITE AMERICAN TO KEEP THE NEGRO INFERIOR AND SUBTERFUGE HIS EVERY ACT ON THE GROUND OF SOCIAL EQUALITY?"

The Washington [D. C.] *Eagle* comments as follows, September 6:

"Social Equality Nonsense

One of the reasons given by Judge Pickle for mobbing Mr. John R. Shillady, the able secretary of the Association for the Advancement of Colored People, in Austin, Tex., in the very shadow of the State capitol, was that he 'advocated and practiced social equality between the races,' and, because of this, 'inciting our Negroes to strife with our white people.' On the face of this statement of the case, without going into the criminal act of mobbing Mr. Shillady, which the governor of the State has condoned as being justifiable, it will be seen that Judge Pickle 'strained at a gnat and swallowed a whale.'

"Social equality rights are personal rights, with which the law does not concern itself. Civil rights are another thing, and the law does concern itself with them. The trouble with Judge Pickle and most Southern people is that they confuse social rights with civil rights. Most of them do not do this ignorantly, but as knowing what they do, and for the purpose of keeping the Afro-American people, however decent and worthy, from the enjoyment of any and all of the civilities and decencies of human society."

.   .   .   .   .

Among the journals that demand "absolute equality," including specifically social equality, *The Guardian* (Boston) is prominent. In almost any issue one might find an utterance, in a reported address or sermon, or in an editorial, such as the following, which is from its columns, July 12:

" 'Another thing upon which Negroes must continue to insist is social equality in every sense of the word. There can be no justice without social equality, because to admit that you are not one's equal in society is to admit that you are entitled to different treatment. What is desired on the part of the white man is that there shall be some evidence of inferiority on the part of the Negro. The four million mulattoes in the United States demonstrate conclusively that there is social equality galore in the United States after dark; and what we want is social equality in the day as well as after dark.' "

From *The Houston Informer*, November 1, I take a large portion of an editorial that treats the subject elaborately and vigorously. It represents, I estimate, ninety-five per cent of the colored press:

"Bosh, Buncombe, 'Bull' 'Bull-sheviki'

What is the idea of all this talk about the colored man or race desiring 'social equality?' What is meant by the employment of that term? Is not the term 'social equality' confused by these disciples of alarm and protectors of the public weal and welfare (most noble scions of democracy!) with the term of 'social intermingling?'

"This stereotyped, antedeluvian and antiquated doctrine has outlived its usefulness and is more the cantankerous cavortings of 'brain-cracked' spotlight seekers and sensational and yellow journalists than it is the earnest and honest convictions and belief of sane and sensible men.

"There is a vast difference between 'social equality' and 'social intermingling.' They are as far apart as the north pole is from the south pole. There can be no justice where equality does not exist.

"What the colored man demands is 'social equity,' 'social sameness.' He wants the same rights of society that other men and races enjoy; but he does not ask the association and companionship of men or women of other races. Social companionship can not be regulated by laws. If Bill Smith wants to associate with John Jones all the laws in the genius of mankind cannot keep them apart.

"On the other hand if they do not desire each other's companionship and comraderie, no law can be enacted that will have sufficient force to compel these two men to be pals or social associates.

"Take both the written and unwritten law of the South relative to 'social intermingling,' what these apostles of alarm and exponents of force and mob-violence are wont to call 'social equality,' and see how recklessly it has been violated and

The Negro's Grievances and Demands 69

trampled upon by men from the other side of the house. Fully 6,000,000 mulattoes out of 14,000,000 colored Americans speak louder than words that somebody is more anxious for 'social intermingling' than the colored race.

"Throughout the South it is very difficult (and this happens quite frequently) to tell which race has a rightful claim upon some of these quadroons and octoroons; in no case is the father of African descent.

"As soon as the colored man asks for a square and fair deal (something the South is unwilling to accord him and will not do until it has to) these monumental hypocrites and camouflagers bring out their age-worn bugbear and bugaboo of 'social equality.' It has been worked so much that it now has the 'wopsy.'

"The South professes and proclaims to the world that it deplores lynch law and is putting forth an earnest effort to blot it out and as soon as colored people organize to aid in combating it, not with force, but through the medium of combined coöperation, the cry is sent broadcast that the 'niggers are organizing for social equality.' And one disgusting part of the entire spectacle is that ofttimes, nowadays, this old tale is started by ex-service men, who are rankling with a spirit of revenge at their colored brothers because the French people treated the latter as men, despite the subtle propaganda of the former.

"The Informer cannot see how any man, who lays any claim to common sense, in the face of the known conditions, can assert in public print or utterance that the black man is trying or the least anxious to cross the line. But he is anxious that men of other races stay on their side of the fence and leave his wife, sisters and daughters alone and that when he protects the sanctity of his home at the hazard of his life, a lyncher's rope will not be his reward.

"All this journalistic diarrhea about 'radical Negro editors' and 'race uplifters inciting Negroes to revolt against the white man,' etc., is unadulterated and unsophisticated bosh, buncombe, 'bull' and 'bull-sheviki.'

"For years the South held both the black man's body and mind in abject bondage; he was treated and regarded as cattle and chattel. When his physical emancipation came a program was immediately launched to retain the black man in mental slavery. He was denied education and military training; forced to live in sections of the towns unfit for hogs and other beasts of the fields; was paid starvation wages and every effort on his part to alter his status was met with stiff and stubborn resistance, even with armed force and other methods of violence and terrorism. All kinds of repressive and oppressive laws were enacted and his every right guaranteed him under both the federal and state constitutions were peremptorily taken away from him and he dared not open his mouth, even in feeble protestation.

"Speaking for the sane, sober-minded and sensible free men of the colored race (we cannot speak for lackeys, stool-pigeons, pimps, parrots, et cetera), the white newspapers need have no fear that members of the colored race are any ways anxious to miscegenate or amalgamate the two races nor is there any desire, even remote, for 'social intermingling,' ' 'n everything.' If the white man will permit our race to remain 100 per cent pure, we shall be perfectly satisfied. Let him take all his illegitimate offspring by black women and colonize them wherever he pleases, remain on his side of the house and then he will have no fear that black men are 'hossing' to be the social companions of white people."

5. *Segregation and Proscription*

Against Jim Crowism—the monster's other name—the colored papers with absolute unanimity utter their imprecations, their sarcastic gibes. In all its protean shapes it is an outrage and an insult, unendurable without protest. Segregation in places of residence, segregation in railway coaches, segregation in theaters, schools, and churches, segregation anywhere, is a sort of spiritual lynching. Not all of these forms are protested against openly in all parts of the country. North of the Ohio River there is outspoken unanimity; south of that river there are, in general, only protests against "discriminations," "unequal accommodations," "inadequate facilities," and the like. Separate schools, for example, are accepted in the South.

Since the dubbing of the up-standing, self-assertive, protesting colored man as "the New Negro," another class, or perhaps the other class, has been dubbed "the Jim Crow Negro." His soul is Jim Crowed. In the race papers' description, he is the hat-in-hand, obsequious, humble-servant type. With abjectness of spirit he accepts Jim Crow cars, Jim Crow schools, Jim Crow hospitals, Jim Crow Y. M. C. A.'s, Jim Crow quarters in the cities, Jim Crow everything. The New Negro of the North will none of these. The New Negro of the South in general but demands equality or equity in these things.

Yet these generalizations, to which there are many exceptions, must be interpreted in the light of the utterances following:

"SOMETHING NEW UNDER THE SUN

CHARLOTTE, N. C., July 22.—Something new under the sun has been found in North Carolina—a 'Jim Crow' postoffice, where Negroes receive their mail from one pigeon hole, and the white people from another. One of Senator Simpson's constituents has sent him a picture showing the dividing line between the white and Colored races at Makatoka, the Jim Crow office."—*Associated Negro Press.*

"About the only things in this world which have no Jim Crow department are nature and death."—*The Vigil* (Norfolk, Va.), October 4.

Incidents of the following order speak for themselves:

STATE CONVENTION OF AMERICAN LEGION IN SESSION AT LEHAM'S HALL. COLORED DELE-GATES REFUSE TO EAT.
.   .   .   .   .   .

"At the annual luncheon of the Convention, the colored delegates were offered seats at a table in a separate room from the others. They refused to eat and to a man walked out and purchased their own lunch elsewhere."—*The Afro-American* (Baltimore), October 10.

"REFUSAL TO ATTEND JIM CROW SCHOOL

Refusal to Attend Jim Crow School in North Causes it to Close Down

Pittsburgh, Pa., Aug. 29, 1919.—The refusal of colored residents to send their children to the separate Negro school,

West Front Street, has forced the school to close down. The parents insisted upon sending their children to the regular public schools with the white children. The opening of this Jim Crow school was widely resented by the colored people and has been unsuccessful from the beginning."—*The Guardian* (Boston), September 13.

"Colored Soldiers of St. Joe, Mo., Resent Snub of Victory Parade Committee

We admire the manhood and grit of the returned colored soldiers of St. Joseph, Mo., who refused to be hung onto the tail end of a Victory parade behind every organization, both military and civic. It was indeed a fine brand of 'World Democracy' as interpreted by the haughty and prejudiced committee on program. The colored soldier could fight abroad for democracy, but could not enjoy the fruits thereof in his own home town.

"The colored band, which was to play up and down the streets during the parade, balked and refused to play on account of the affront shown the Race. Hurrah for them too and give three cheers for Dr. Carrion who had enough iron in his blood to tell the white folks that there was a new Negro on the stage of action who would at all times expect the treatment due a real man and that he would govern himself accordingly."
—*The Wichita Protest.*

The *Hot Springs Echo* thus notes the discrimination against colored soldiers in Arkansas:

"The American Legion which met in state convention at Little Rock this week, among other things voted to bar Negroes from representation in state conventions, but authorizing the organization of sub-posts in each county under authority of local posts.

"It was voted that only white men shall be eligible as delegates to the national convention."

Then, in this paper's way, little gibes like these are sprinkled over the editorial page:

"The American Legion was not so particular about its complexion being 'lily-white' when it came to 'looking the Germans in the eye.'

"For valor displayed in the recent war, it seems that the Negro's particular decoration is to be the 'double cross.'"

From *The Forum* (Springfield, Ill.), October 18, I take this editorial, which deals with several phases of the subject of segregation:

"Segregation is carried out effectively in the South, even to the cemetery, where mortal man is popularly supposed to be unable to have any intercourse and therefore no friction can be caused. But they have more trouble in the South with all the thorough practice of segregation than is had in the North where it is not carried to such extremes. The white people of the South say that the Negroes are satisfied, and the colored people leave by the thousands monthly. Thus we see that in spite of the segregation and repression, the problem continues and will continue until all reach and put into practice a standard of valuation based on something other than color or previous condition.

"A bad theory is better than none at all, and the Negro problem is so fascinating that almost every person has some sort of panacea to proffer as a solution. But very few suggest directly according the Negro the same treatment as a white man, and measured by the same standard of value. The reason is quite apparent—it is unpopular. Here lies the crux of the whole question; the white people endeavor to solve the 'problem' according to preconceived ideas regardless of justice and based, for the major portion, on fallacies.

"The average white man thinks that the Negro wants to marry white women—from whence this notion sprung, we are unable to state, and all his reasoning revolves around this one thing that he accepts as a fact."

The spiritual aspect of segregation is touched upon in this editorial from *The Planet* (Richmond), August 30:

"Intermixing is not the cause and segregation and restriction are not the remedy. I know not what is meant by 'absorption into the common stock by intermarriage,' but Atlanta was segregated and so were East Saint Louis, Chicago and Washington, if not by law, by custom. Wherefore, then, the riots?

"It is not to be expected that a mutual, basic understanding will ever obtain between the ignorant blacks and whites, North or South, but aloofness and lack of genuine understanding between the better element of thinkers—the controlling element—of the two peoples are the underlying cause of race friction.

"Intelligent, give-and-take coöperative committee work between the sober-minded whites and blacks is the remedy; and until that day dawns we may expect, in fact we invite, racial upheavals in the future which may surpass in gruesomeness even Atlanta, East Saint Louis, Washington and Chicago. It is to be a curse on no particular section, but will blight every inch of American soil where ignorance is rampant and uncontrolled. Will somebody step forward and make the first move for God and Humanity?"

V. RIOTS.

FREQUENT reference was made in the colored papers during the summer to early riots in Charleston, Atlanta, Norfolk, Longview, and elsewhere in the Southern states. It was not, however, until the riot in the nation's capital that national interest was aroused. The riot in Chicago intensified that interest. Then followed the Knoxville riot, the Omaha riot, the Elaine riot, with a few minor clashes hardly noticed in the general situation. Beginning with Longview, my extracts will deal with these race conflicts in the order in which they are here named.

1. *Longview*

"INSIDE INFORMATION ABOUT RACE RIOT AT LONGVIEW, TEXAS

Longview, Tex., July 12.—Nearly two hundred members of the Texas National Guard from Dallas and Nacogdoches, ordered here to-day by Governor W. P. Hobby to prevent further clashes between whites and Negroes, were arriving to-night by train and automobiles.

"The trouble to-day occurred when the white men were waylaid and fired upon in the Negro section of Longview, where they had gone in search of F. L. Jones, a Negro school teacher, accused of causing the publication of the story in The Chicago Defender of the lynching of Lemuel Walters at Longview on June 17. The story ran that 'Walters was lynched when a prominent white woman declared she loved him and that if she were in the North, she would get a divorce and marry him.'

"The whites returned the fire of the Negroes, who were hidden in vantage points, and withdrew when their ammunition was exhausted, four of their number having suffered wounds.

"A general alarm was sounded and the whites, with reinforcements, returned to the scene, to find that the Negroes had dispersed. Five of the principal Negro residences were then burned by the whites. Local officials, unable to cope with the situation, called upon the Governor for aid."—*The Associated Negro Press,* July 12.

Other accounts in the colored press told of the flogging in the public streets of the colored school principal, "a high class, educated, Christian gentleman," and the driving from the community several prominent colored citizens.

2. *Washington*

The riot in our national capital, July 19 and 20, doubtless made too deep an impression upon the public mind to have as yet been forgotten. But how the Negro viewed that riot, what to him the causes of it were, who the instigators and real rioters were, doubtless it never occurred to one white person in a hundred thousand to consult a Negro paper to discover. Their answers to those questions are here given. The first pronouncement is from two of the most conservative Negro leaders in the country, and men of eminent abilities, who gave to the press of the country a statement of which the essential purport is contained in these extracts:

"CAPITAL MIXUP IS EXPLAINED

Letters and telegrams from Colored people throughout the country have come to us and to others of our Race here in Washington from all parts of the country, revealing widespread unrest and agitation among the thoughtful leaders of the Negro people, who sense a growing feeling of suspicion as between the races at a time when there should be amity, concord and mutual respect and confidence.

"We believe that we express the opinion of the leading men and women of this community when we say that the Colored people of the District of Columbia are not responsible for the deplorable conditions which have existed during the past week. We do not hesitate to say that the responsibility for this unfortunate riot lies primarily at the door of the mob composed of white men—soldiers, sailors and marines—which ran amuck through the streets of the national capital, maiming, injuring and killing innocent Colored citizens a week ago. The retaliation which followed on the part of the Colored people, although to be deplored, was, under the circumstances, but natural.

. . . .

"We call upon the law-abiding members of the Negro race everywhere to coöperate with their white fellow citizens in all efforts to repress mob violence, to the end that men who shared the sacrifices and hardships of the late war, as well as all other members of our Race, may mutually share in the finer rewards which should come out of a fair settlement of the reconstruction and readjustment problems which face us on every side.

"Men of both races should set their faces against further clashes of this character in every part of our country."

Emmet J. Scott (Secretary-Treasurer Howard University).

R. H. Terrell (Judge Municipal Court, Washington, D. C.).

The following special article in *The Call* (Kansas City, Mo.), will further indicate where the Negro placed the blame for this and succeeding riots, and what attitude was universally taken toward assaults, "mis-called riots":

"Hell seems to have broken loose in Washington, D. C., within the past few weeks, and the vicious and malignant type of the white race which is temporarily domiciled there has given fresh proof of its insensate, and unreasoning prejudice to Negro advancement, and of its own crass ignorance and narrowness. These outbreaks of the mob in Washington and Chicago have taught it one thing which it will not soon forget, viz.: That the Negro MEANS to be as merciless in repelling attacks upon him as the attackers. The NEW NEGRO, unlike the old time Negro, 'does not fear the face of clay,' and the white man will learn in time that he has in this new type of Negro a foeman worthy of his steel. The time for cringeing is over. If we are driven to defend our lives, our homes, our rights either by responsible or irresponsible mobs, let us do it MAN FASHION. Since it is appointed unto all men once to die, how better can we die than in defending our lives, our homes, our rights from the attacks of white men obsessed with the idea that this world was made for Cæsar and his queens.

"The newspapers in other sections of the country (some of them) have attempted to justify these riots on the ground that Negroes in Washington attempted to rape white women. A more vicious and cowardly libel on the Negroes of Washington was never uttered. The Negroes of Washington, D. C., have for more than a hundred years maintained a reputation for law and order, and respect for womanhood unequaled by the Negroes of any other section of the country. That they have now suddenly developed into rapists with a penchant for second or third class white women will not be believed even by the liars who make the charge to divert attention from the real cause of these outbreaks."

In the section on *The White Press* information was given about the alleged attacks upon white women by Negroes. Articles that follow will indicate the universal Negro view of these stories.

The perennial contention regarding Negro assaults upon white women as the cause of lynchings and riots, and the shielding of the guilty by their own race, is in evidence in the following editorial from *The Southwestern Christian Advocate* (New Orleans). It is one of many such defenses combined with recrimination. This article was called forth by the accusation in a white denominational weekly that Negro editors, while deploring mob violence, fail to denounce the crimes that provoke the mob. After denying this charge vigorously the colored editor continues:

"Let Us Look at the Facts Squarely

We do want to call attention, however, specifically to the claim that the Washington riots followed 'assaults upon white women by Negroes.' It has been very clearly proven that there was no series of assaults. To use the strongest language possible there were only attempted 'assaults.' These attempted assaults were mere approaches, the motive for which is not perfectly clear. There was only one Negro who made the approach upon four women. Three of these women were not hurt. The fourth woman was colored; she was of such fair complexion that she was mistaken for white and the Negro who made the assault and the papers who exploited assault were likewise deceived. We have wondered quite often that if the newspapers of Washington knew that this fair skinned woman was colored whether they would have made such a howl about this particular assault as they did.

"According to the records of the Washington Police Department there occurred in the District of Columbia during the month preceding the riot one case of rape and two cases of attempt at rape on white women.

"This leads us into another field.

"Mark you, we do not intend, much less attempt, to condone or underestimate the hideousness and the awfulness of assault by Negroes upon white women, but we do wonder how people of such sensitiveness for the condemnation of assault against womanhood cannot be aroused the least bit when Negro women are assaulted. It seems as if virtue is a matter of color. Right at the bottom of the whole thing is this lack of consideration of Negro womanhood and much of the trouble in our inter-racial life lies right here. Negro womanhood must be made sacred and respected and we avow that white men who assault Negro womanhood (and there are thousands of them) are no less brutes and should be frowned upon no less than those to whom is meted out punishment for their crimes."

3. *Chicago*

A week after the Washington riot a still more violent one occurred in Chicago. The two following articles will supplement each other. The first is from one of the Chicago weeklies of which I have lost the reference:

"How the Trouble Started

Chicago, Ill., July 28.—The scene of Riot has shifted from Washington, the nation's capital, to Chicago, America's greatest cosmopolitan city, and regarded everywhere as the world's greatest center of race progress. Sunday afternoon, a colored lad was bathing in Lake Michigan near the beach at East Twenty-ninth Street. The day was hot and tens of thousands of Chicago's population were seeking relief from the heat in the cooling waters of Lake Michigan. This lad was on a raft and a white ruffian threw a stone and knocked him into

the water where he drowned before ᴜeing ɾescued. The attention of white policemen was immediately called to the ruffian,
but the policeman refused to arrest the man, whereupon the
crowd became angered and in a short time began to "clean up"
the place. The man accused of the crime is Augusta Strauber.
Finally he was arrested by two colored detectives, Middleton
and Scott. The news of the crime scattered like wild fire.
Hundreds rushed from the beach in their bathing costumes,
hurrying to places of shelter while others hurried to their
nearby homes for revolvers and rifles. And, in less than an
hour, there was a general battle in which more than one
hundred whites were injured by weapons of various kinds."

The strife spread, and the violence, attended by the burning
of large districts and the killing and wounding of many people,
continued for a day or two.

In regard to the genesis of this riot, the following account,
from the pen of Lucian B. Watkins in *The Planet* (Richmond,
Va.), October 25, gives additional history further back:

"Let me make this the first sentence of what I have to say:
THE PRIMARY CAUSE OF THE TROUBLES BE-
TWEEN THE WHITE AND BLACK RACES IN AMER-
ICA IS THE INBORN HATRED THAT IS IN THE
HEARTS OF THOSE WHO RESENT THE HUMAN AS-
PIRATIONS OF COLORED PEOPLE. This Satanic germ
was conceived and hatched in the souls of slave-holders and is
only bearing its dreadly fruit, after its kind. Race-hatred
prompted the crimes against Colored people, in Chicago, that
were perpetrated immediately preceding the riots: The repeated
bombing of the homes of Colored citizens; the inexcusable
beating of those Colored men and women in Washington Park,
last June; the murder of that Colored man at Fifty-fourth
Street and Wentworth Avenue; another at Fifty-seventh Street
and Lafayette Avenue; then the stoning and consequent
drowning of that black boy, at the beach. Race-hatred tole-
rated the escape from apprehension of these murderers, and
was the sympathy shown toward the murderer in the last-
mentioned case. While Chicago's white policemen, with their
white soldier assistants, were busy disarming the Colored people, during the riots, Chief of Police John J. Garrity, advised
the white people to arm themselves. This significant news

appeared in one of Chicago's leading white newspapers. Race-hatred was the monster who arrested the 'rioters'; more than 200 Colored and less than 100 white. The riots were started by a white offender, at the beach; white mobs invaded the colored residential sections, and the victims of their number were killed by the colored defendants of their own lives, property and homes; the deaths, resulting from the riots, are officially recorded as 23 colored and 15 white; of the colored killed, it has been proven that seven met their deaths at the hands of the police and their helpers. Pursuing its foul policy, race-hatred promptly charged the outraged colored people with having caused the onslaught of the hoodlum white mobs. And it seems that the worst is not yet come."

The Negroes, in reviewing the incidents of the various riots, exulted in the courage and sacrificial deeds of members of their race. *The Chicago Defender,* August 9, affords an example:

"Heroic Deeds Told

Space will not permit the covering of the complete story of all the worthy activities put forth by various members of our Race in this our greatest crisis. There were a number of commendable things observed by both citizens and officials of our Race which will go down in history as worthy examples of Race pride, loyalty and devotion and unparalleled bravery and heroism. Officers John T. Scott, William Middleton, M. P. Parker, in company with ex-Alderman Oscar DePriest, made several trips during the fiercest of the fray in affected districts and relieved Colored families who were surrounded by those who sought their lives and sought to destroy their homes. Of all the men who appeared in the public press speaking for our people, none spoke with calmer judgment and greater deliberation than Edward H. Wright, assistant corporation counsel. With few exceptions the thinking men of our Race were of one accord, and sought to do everything in their power to allay race feeling and hatred and resentment. A few unworthy examples were evidenced by men who sought attention in the public press as a means to rehabilitate their lost honor and respect. They are unworthy of mentioning."

The colored people of Chicago protested loudly against State's Attorney Hoyne, accusing him of favoring the whites and demanding his removal or that the prosecution of the rioters be taken out of his hands. The following is the first half of an editorial in *The Chicago Defender*, September 6:

"Mr. Hoyne's Mistaken View

STATE'S ATTORNEY HOYNE it seems is of the impression that Colored gamblers started the race riots in Chicago. Mr. Hoyne is mistaken. He fails absolutely to grasp the underlying causes of the race clashes in this community. When he charges our people with having brought on the disgraceful happenings centering about the first week of August, he flies in the face of the real facts.

"MR. HOYNE seems to have lost sight of a number of very disagreeable instances immediately preceding the actual outbreak of hostilities between whites and blacks. He has forgotten, evidently, the repeated bombing of the homes of our citizens, resulting in the destruction of much valuable property. Likewise he overlooks the wanton and inexcusable beatings of our men and women in Washington Park about the middle of June. His memory also proves false when he fails to call to mind that a Colored man was killed at Fifty-fourth and Union avenue, another at Fifty-first and Wentworth avenue, and still another at Fifty-seventh and Lafayette avenue. All of these things happened prior to the outbreaks of the latter part of July and the first of August.

"HAS OUR STATE'S ATTORNEY FORGOTTEN that not a single miscreant responsible for these murders has been apprehended? Is it to be wondered at that in the face of such laxity on the part of those charged with law enforcement that Colored citizens, in their alarm, should have sought and applied drastic measures for their own protection? While it is true that the hoodlum element may have been guilty of many overt acts, it is also true that the respectable element among our citizens were impelled to go outside of the law to protect themselves and their property when they could see no help from constituted authority.

"WE CAN EASILY UNDERSTAND the indictment of so many of our group. The conduct of the police force, in many instances, lends strong color to the suspicion that they were more or less in sympathy with the white rioters. It is only fair to deduce this from the fact that so many of our people were arrested in striking contrast to the arrest of the few white persons participating in the rioting. Even the grand jury, composed of some of Chicago's leaders in business and society, were forced to take note of this one-sided phase of the situation."

4. *Knoxville*

Regarding the Knoxville riot, August 30-31, I select the first part of an editorial from *The Planet* (Richmond, Va.), September 6:

"The Riot at Knoxville

Some worthless colored man was accused of approaching Mrs. Bertie Lindsey, a white lady in her home at Knoxville, Tenn., and in her fright in running away from him she killed herself. This was conveyed to the public as an assault by a Negro upon a white woman and when a colored man suspected of the offense was landed in jail, a mob formed and attempted to break into the jail and lynch the accused man without a trial. As a result of this action more than a score of people have been injured, some of them fatally, thousands of dollars expended for troops, fifty thousand dollars' worth of property destroyed and the good name of the community irreparably injured.

"It would seem that this is convincing testimony that mob-law does not pay. In the meantime, the man guilty of the offense has not been punished and at this time, it is not at all certain that he is even under arrest, although a man is being placed on trial to prove his innocence.

"It is a noticeable fact that the mob leaders broke into the jail and proceeded to loot the supply of liquor held there. They seemed to be more anxious to secure the liquor than they were the persons guilty of crime, for they released old offenders, men who had committed felonies."

The following editorials will fully represent the Negro's version and interpretation of the facts of this riot:

"SOLDIERS RIOT

Mobbism in Knoxville

Brutalities and indignities to which colored people were subjected in Knoxville, Tenn., made it necessary for citizens, both white and colored, to petition Governor Roberts to order white soldiers removed from that city.

"The soldiers sent to check the mob that attacked the jail here on the night of August 30, and liberated all the white prisoners, did almost as much harm as the mob. A false report was circulated to the effect that Negroes had killed two white men. This was done to turn the attention of the soldiers from the mob at the jail. The soldiers, hearing this report, rushed into the colored section with a machine gun and began firing. As a result, one colored man and one of the officers commanding the soldiers were killed.

"The soldiers were given orders by some one to search and disarm all the Negroes. A more disgraceful order was never issued. From 4 o'clock Sunday morning until night, colored men and women were stopped on the streets and searched by the soldiers. Nothing more than pocketknives were found on them, but the soldiers took the knives from them. One colored man going three blocks was searched seven times. The indignities which colored women suffered at the hands of these soldiers would make the devil blush for shame. Low class white men took advantage of the helplessness of the colored men and began cursing and abusing them on the streets. One colored man, coming home with his family, was struck and humiliated by a white ruffian."—*The Call* (Kansas City, Mo.), October 4.

"More of the Fruits of Lawlessness

The Knoxville riot adds emphasis to a fact which has already been proclaimed to the country by the Washington and the Chicago riots: The Negro will no longer allow himself to be mobbed free of cost. Those who indulge in mobbing him now and hereafter have got to pay the cost, and pay it in lives.

"There are lots of white people who are holding up their hands in horror at this state of mind in which the race now is, people who have never held up their hands even in deprecation at the beating and killing and shooting and hanging and burning alive of Negroes by mobs. And there are some colored people, timid souls, who are greatly distressed over what seems to be a sudden turn about in the attitude of the race.

"The race as a whole is not worried and will not be deterred by either set of people. Deep down in its consciousness is a grim determination, the determination that when unprotected by the law it will defend itself against the mob, and do so to the death.

"The Negro has tried every other expedient. He has been humble, he has been patient and long suffering, he has prayed to God and he has petitioned the Government; now he has determined when death at the hands of a mob confronts him, to stand in his tracks and die like a man and not like a hunted animal."—*The New York Age*, September 6.

Regarding the trial of the Knoxville rioters, *The East Tennessee News* (Knoxville), October 30, made this announcement:

"Jury's Verdict a Surprise

The rioters that were charged with felonies in breaking into the Knox county jail and releasing many murderers and desperate criminals were placed on trial in criminal court. There were twenty-two in number and the trial resulted in all having been acquitted with the exception of five whose cases resulted in a mistrial."

5. *Omaha*

"Omaha, Neb., Sept. 30.—After a night of mob rule during which a Negro was lynched, an attempt made to hang the mayor of Omaha, Edward P. Smith, the county court house burned, one man, said to be an ex-soldier, shot and killed, and perhaps forty others injured, the city was quiet to-day under patrol of federal troops ordered from Fort Omaha and Fort Crok.

MAYOR IN HOSPITAL

"The mayor is at a hospital and was still unconscious early to-day as a result of the attempt made by the mob to hang him to a trolley pole, because he advised against the lynching of William Brown, a negro, who was in the county jail charged with attacking a white girl on the outskirts of the city early last week.

"With dawn to-day, Omaha's downtown section looked well nigh a wreck as the result of the rioting. Practically all the known casualties that were not fatal, resulted from shooting. Thousands of shots were fired from various kinds of weapons, all discharged in the open with thousands of people on the streets.

"The fire that was started in the court house left that magnificent structure a mass of ruins. The property was valued at a million and a half dollars. The damage to the records could not be estimated early to-day, but it is believed many have been destroyed beyond reclamation. Statistics vital to county officials since the county was organized are believed to be badly damaged.

TURNED NEGRO OVER

"For several hours the lives of more than 100 prisoners in the county jail were endangered by the flames in the lower floors of the building. It was finally necessary to send them all to the roof. Sheriff Clark stood off the angry mob until the flames caused the prisoners themselves to take action. They at first decided among themselves to throw the negro from the roof to the pavement below and leave him to the destruction of the mob. It was at this moment that the mob that had gained entrance to the burning building pushed past Sheriff Clark and his deputies and forced their way into the cell corridor. Here it was the negro was turned over to them.

"Throwing a rope around his neck, these men, numbering about fifty, dragged him to the ground floor, down stifling stairways and through blinding smoke to the street. When they appeared at the Harney Street entrance to the court house they were greeted by a howling mob of thousands.

NEGRO WAS DEAD

"Brown was practically dead before his form was even strung to the light pole. Two bullets were fired into his body as he was dragged through the crowd. He was never heard to utter a word and he was not given an opportunity to speak before being stretched full length before the gaze of thousands.

"Brown's body was mutilated beyond recognition of a human being. Riddled by a thousand bullets, it was first placed over a fire of tarred fagots. It was not permitted to remain there long, however, as it was soon being dragged through the streets at the end of a rope pulled by fifty members of the mob. This spectacle did not end until late in the morning hours when what remained of the torso was hung to a trolley pole at one of the most important downtown intersections."—*The Wichita* [Kansas] *Protest.*

As regards alleged Negro assaults upon white women, something was quoted in the section on the White Press. The following article further elucidates the case as between the whites and the blacks of Omaha in respect to assaults upon women:

"Negroes and Assault

It has been given wide publicity that assaults and attempted assaults by Negroes upon white women and girls had so inflamed the public mind that summary vengeance was inevitable. It is true that there have been many reports in the press of such crimes, some of which when run to earth were found to be groundless or unsubstantiated. The report of County Attorney Shotwell on the status of assault cases which was given to the press last Saturday throws a rather startling and unexpected light upon the situation, which should have a sobering effect upon those who are disposed to believe that Negroes are chief offenders in the commission of this heinous crime. It is a matter of record that there are now awaiting trial in district court seventeen persons held for this crime. Of this number FOUR are Negroes and THIRTEEN are WHITE MEN! One, a white man, Alfred J. Ramsey, who was accused of attempted assault upon a sixteen-year-old colored girl, was found not guilty by a jury, and Jerry Dennis, a Negro, is serving a term in the penitentiary for attempted assault upon a young white woman. No Negro accused of this crime has been admitted to bail, and only three white men accused of attempted assault have been released under heavy bonds."—*The Monitor* (Omaha), October 9.

6. *Elaine*

In October the white press of the country carried alarming reports of a Negro conspiracy in Phillips County, Arkansas, to massacre the whites. Reports of rioting followed. The Negro version of that lamentable affair is something very different from those reports, as the following typical articles will show.

"Race Clash In Phillips Co.

As the result of a very serious clash this week between the races in Phillips County, eastern Arkansas, the deaths up to Friday morning were placed at 22; five whites and seventeen Negroes. The cause of the outbreak is said to have been due to propaganda spread among the Negro citizens of Phillips County which urged them to hold secret meetings, and to demand certain prices for their cotton and labor. It appears that certain well known Negroes were busy organizing the Negro farmers to hold their products for higher prices, not to work for planters unless they received the wage demanded and to organize for their own protection. It is also stated that the Negroes were influenced to adopt a defiant and independent attitude upon the advice of a white lawyer, who had been retained by 68 or more tenant farmers to look after their interests in securing proper settlement of claims against white planters. Many whites knew of the conditions which had been brewing at Elaine and in the surrounding country for two weeks or more; that the Negroes were organizing to demand special prices for labor; to hold their products, etc."— *The Hot Springs Echo,* October 4.

"SYSTEMATIC ROBBERY CAUSE OF RIOTS

ARKANSAS NEGROES HAD NOT PLANNED MASSACRE

The cause of the disturbances in Arkansas was systematic robbery of Negro tenant farmers and share croppers. For years Negroes have been working the farms of white owners on shares and when the time came for a settlement, owners have refused to give them itemized statements of their accounts. Negro tenant farmers and share croppers must buy their supplies during the year from the plantation store or some designated store. The system kept the Negro continually in debt and it is an unwritten law in Arkansas as in many parts of the South that the Negro may not leave the plantation until the debt is paid.

" 'The Progressive Farmers and Household Union of America' was formed by Negro share croppers and the dues paid were to go into a common fund to employ a lawyer. The lawyer was to make a test case in court of one tenant farmer's inability to obtain an itemized statement of his account.

"On October 6 tenant farmers on 21 plantations were to ask

Riots   89

the owners for a settlement. It appears that, failing a settlement, the Negroes were going to refuse to pick the cotton then in the field or to sell cotton belonging to them for less than the market price. Trouble, however, was precipitated when W. A. Adkins, a special agent for the Missouri Pacific Railroad, Charles Pratt, a deputy sheriff and a Negro 'trusty' were fired upon, so it is claimed, by Negroes in a church at Hoop Spur. Adkins was killed and Pratt severely wounded. A statement of one of the persons in the church at the time, however, shows that Adkins and Pratt fired into the church without provocation and that their fire was returned with the above-mentioned results. That precipitated the trouble.

"One case which will show the economic exploitation is that of a Negro on the plantation of R. B. McCombs, a white man in Ashley County, Arkansas. The Negro's crop was worth $3,322.76, the Negro's share being $1,661.38. McCombs paid the Negro $326 and refused to pay him any more, declaring that the Negro had taken up the balance in goods. The Negro brought suit but failed to obtain a judgment, the jury being white, as is always the case in that part of the country.

"Another Negro coming from the State Labor Commissioner's office declared that he had worked 27 acres on shares and that the total value of his crop at present prices was $1,506. The owner of the land had taken all of the crop, had refused a settlement and the Negro had walked 122 miles to Little Rock hoping to get a lawyer, being absolutely penniless. Many similar cases could be cited and it was a determination to protest these conditions that led to the formation of the organization which is claimed by the whites to have 'planned a massacre.'

"So far as I was able to discover, after a careful investigation on the ground, there is no basis for belief that a massacre was planned by Negroes and, in point of fact, it was the Negroes who were massacred.

"Negroes outnumber whites 6 to 1 in Phillips County and if a massacre had been planned the casualty list would not have been 25 Negroes as against 5 whites.

"Many white people expressed doubt of the truth of the 'massacre' stories sent out. It appears that the purpose of those stories was to cloak the robbery of Negroes by white landlords and agents. Prices charged by landlords and plantation stores as compared with those in open market: Bacon (cheapest grade, known as sour belly) plantation 50c lb.;

open market 20c lb. Mary Jane Molasses, plantation $2.00 gal.; open market $1.10 gal. Compound lard, plantation 56c lb.; open market 28c lb. Sack of flour 24 lb., plantation $2.50; open market $1.25.

"In one case a Negro was charged $50 for two second-hand plows which cost, when new, $16 each. In another case, a set of rope plow lines which cost 25c each were sold for $3.50 to the Negro. In another case a Negro was charged $58 for a tow sack and 4 bushels of cotton seed, the value of which was $4.00. In another case a Negro was charged $52.50 express for moving of nine pieces of furniture 100 miles by freight. The actual cost could not have been over $5.00.

"There have been numerous lynchings in the past when Negroes have attempted to obtain settlements from landlords and the farmers' organization was a combine for the purpose of protesting such outrageous conditions as these."—*The Savannah Tribune,* October 23.

In each of these riots—which the colored press denominated mob-assaults and pogroms—there were incidents specially featured. Heroes and martyrs are commemorated. The outstanding incident of the "Arkansas pogrom" was the slaying of the Johnston brothers. From *The National Defender and Sun* (Gary, Ind.), October 25, I take an article that appeared in substance throughout the colored press:

"ALMOST ENTIRE JOHNSTON FAMILY IS MURDERED BY FIENDISH HELL-HOUNDS OF ARKANSAS

(Special to the Defender and Sun.)

Helena, Ark., Oct. 24.—The report that the four Johnston brothers who were outrageously murdered near Elaine, Ark., met death in a riot at the latter place, is not true. The four brothers, one of whom, Dr. L. H. Johnston of Cowweta, Okla., who was there visiting his other brothers, had been hunting and were peacefully returning home with their game when they were intercepted by a white man, supposed to be a friend of the Johnston boys, and told that a race riot was in progress in Elaine and advised them not to go in that direction, but to return to a point below Elaine, leave their guns to avoid suspicion, and take the train for Helena. After considerable persuasion on the part of their supposed white friend, the Johnstons followed his advice, trying to avoid trouble that they knew nothing of. When the train on which they were riding en route to Helena reached Elaine, their good white 'friend' led a mob aboard the Jim Crow coach and with guns drawn commanded the Johnston boys to throw up their hands, according to eye-witnesses, and in a few seconds had handcuffed three of the boys, evidently not recognizing Dr. L. H. Johnston as one of the brothers, and was marching them out of the train when Doctor Johnston spoke to the men, saying: 'Gentlemen, these men are my brothers, and I want to know why you are taking them from this train.' In reply, one of the men said: 'If you are their brother you'd better come along with them.' To this Dr. L. H. Johnston retorted: 'Well, I will certainly go,' whereupon he was handcuffed, and the four forced at the point of guns to get in a waiting auto and hurriedly driven off. That night about eleven o'clock the bodies of the four brothers, riddled with bullets and mutilated with knives or other sharp instruments, were found by the roadside. They had been murdered in cold blood!

"The perpetrators of this gruesome atrocity then issued a statement to the effect that one of the Johnstons took a gun from a deputy sheriff and killed him, causing the posse to fire on the four brothers, killing all of them instantly.

"Mrs. Mercy Johnston, mother of the unfortunate quartette, who lived in Chicago in a home purchased for her by her sons, was at the time in Pine Bluff, visiting relatives. She accompanied by relatives and friends, her heart all but breaking over the sad occurence, went to claim the bodies of her loved ones, that she might at least pay a mother's last tribute, even though that should be in tears and heartache, but rank insult was added to injury when she was compelled to pay a ransom for the dead bodies. She paid the price, however, and followed the remains to their last resting place in Little Rock. The funeral was the biggest and most impressive ever seen in that city. No man was quite strong enough to look upon this terrible scene. The great wonder is that any black should witness such a scene and be free from that which makes men desperate."

The trial of the accused Negroes in the Elaine trouble, as reported by the colored press, was a travesty upon justice.

The majority of those brought into court were given to understand that if they pleaded guilty of murder in the second degree they would be let off with penitentiary sentences. The result may be guessed. Each trial lasted six or seven minutes, no witnesses for the defense being heard. Seventy-five Negroes were given penitentiary terms ranging from five to twenty-one years; twelve were sentenced to the electric chair.

Efforts to secure a new trial were unavailing. But finally execution was postponed and the Supreme Court of Arkansas ordered a stay of execution. The colored people throughout America at this date (January 20, 1920), are raising a defense fund. Petitions are being sent to the National Government for a federal investigation. The colored press continues to have much to say by way of protest, denunciation, and exposure on the subject. The following brief article is typical:

"TRUTH SLIPS OUT

ARKANSAS STILL WASHES DIRTY LINEN

Little Rock, Ark., Dec. 30, 1919.—Rumors are afloat here and in and about Helena and Elaine, that point the accusing finger towards white men as the real murderers of the planters in and about Elaine, for which several score of Negroes have been convicted, some of whom having been condemned to die.

"The rumors that are whispered are to the effect that soon there will be suits instituted in the courts to collect damages from men who are charged with being local representatives of a syndicate, that has for a long time been trying to secure land holdings in and about Elaine. The finger points to the filing of these white planters by local white men who are now trying to secure title to the property of the deceased.

"Dame rumor continues to show that when the whole thing is sifted, there will be disclosed a well defined and organized effort to commit wholesale murder and hide the crime behind the usual southern goat, the black man. Thousands of Negroes have left this section to the extent that it is causing a serious economic disturbance, and the out-pouring still continues. The relatives of the Johnston brothers have not yet received any portion of the insurance on the lives of the slain black men, the insurance company withholding payment until an examination can be had of the contention of the relatives to the effect that the sheriff, who had the Johnston boys in charge, killed them." —*The Black Dispatch* (Oklahoma City), January 2, 1920.

On the subject of lawlessness and riots generally some editorial expressions seem appropriate. The following editorial is of a type that is common in the smaller Southern papers. It is from *The Hot Springs Echo*, October 4:

"Is It Fair and Just

An irresponsible or criminally inclined black man commits a serious offense:

"Whites generally, do not as a rule satisfy themselves with bringing him to swift legal account and just punishment:

"But only the remark needs to be made that 'Negroes are too bigoted anyhow and need to be taught a lesson':

"This inflammatory remark soon spreads and whites whose minds are already impregnated with the seeds of prejudice begin to murmur:

"The murmur increases in volume and grows into a roar:

"It is the voice of the mob:

"Then incendiary speeches, adding fuel to the flames of race hatred:

"Leaders urge destruction:

"Attack is begun upon every human whose face is black. Matters not if a colored man has labored hard for 20 or 30 years to build up a good name and to establish a trustworthy record in the community; to obey the laws; accumulate property and live a life of usefulness:

"The mob sees only that his color is black; he is a Negro and therefore an object for attack and annihilation. The peaceful, law-abiding Negro is forced to flee for his life and when cornered, to fight for it. If he survives and escapes he is an outlaw; if he surrenders himself to the law he is taken as a rioter; a murderer and must spend his little substance trying to avoid spending a large portion of his life in penal servitude:

"God help his wife and children.

"Fair-minded white citizens and friends must admit that these conditions are true. We ask are such things fair and just?

"How long, O Lord, ere the change comes?"

From a dozen or a score of similar editorials I select this as perhaps fairly representing the voice of the Negro. It is from *The Savannah Tribune:*

"The Country Aflame

Sporadic outbursts of mob violence are bound to continue so long as the guardians of the legislatures and the laws will temporize with lawbreakers and those who would destroy our civilization.

"Indulgence of first offenses against the fundamentals of citizenship, the minor invasions of personal and property rights, merely because they were directed against Negroes, has brought about a general wanton and lawless state of mind as regards these things, and riot and bloodshed are the only logical consequences.

"The South has never accepted nor acquiesced in the amendments to the Constitution of the United States insuring and securing Negro citizenship and civil and political equality. Lynching and other forms of oppression are meant to deter Negroes from insisting on compliance with these fundamental laws. Thousands of subterfuges and adroit circumventions have been employed in the South to protect those charged with executing the law in their discrimination. All this the Northern whites have suffered or acquiesced in.

"More and more as Negroes develop to appreciate the advantages of civilization and come to feel more and more keenly the disappointment arising from an abridgement of their common rights, more and more will there be occasions for conflict.

"Unless the firm hand of the national government intervenes to establish the peaceful relationship that should exist between the white and black people throughout the country, we shall not stop until anarchy and riot rule the land.

"This is no new story. The present storm of race hate has not broken in surprise. We have seen the clouds gathering and thickening for many days. A thousand communities are on edge to-day, because each furnishes the fuel to kindle the fires of riot and bloodshed. In Georgia a lynching was kept out of the newspapers for over two months. A community is depraved and demoralized when snch a thing can take place. Thousands of Negroes all over the country, particularly in farming communities, are living in a state of terror and apprehension for safety of their lives.

"It is getting to be a dangerous thing to acquire property, to get an education, to own an automobile, to dress well, and to build a respectable home.

"Who can dispute this in the face of the slaughter of industrious Negroes like the Goolsbys at Blakely, the Scotts at Millen, the seven Negroes in Brooks and Lowndes Counties, Anthony Crawford, and others? Most of the Negroes lynched are prosperous and industrious nowadays.

"If any one can deny, let him speak!"

For the fullest summary at hand of the whole matter from the Negro's point of view the following elaborate statement from *The Houston Informer,* October 25, must be read. It will not bear abridgement.

"Some Light On Rapes, Lynchings and Riots; Facts and Figures Cited

The Houston Chronicle opines that 'the causes of lynchings are already well known; and the remedy for lynchings is in the hands of the colored people themselves.' It then gives as the cause for lynchings and riots 'the crime of rape of white women by lecherous black brutes.'

"The famous Southern daily charges that 'the colored people themselves try to protect and shield the perpetrator of that crime, and in the event of his capture band together to employ counsel and use money in an attempt to get him clear.'

"It is an age-worn and over-worked lie of the deepest dye.

"Let us deal in facts and figures for a while, so that such damnable and insidious propaganda can be shown up in its real form.

"There have been five so-called race riots during this year, viz: Longview, Texas; Washington, D. C.; Chicago, Ill.; Knoxville, Tenn.; Elaine, Ark. The Omaha, Neb., affair was not a race riot, but a lynching fest.

"Of the five alleged race riots, rape was only assigned by the white press (mind you) in one case and that was the Washington affair. Yet, according to the data of Major Pullman, Washington's chief of police, there occurred in that city between June 25, 1919, and the outbreak of the riot, ONE

CASE OF RAPE and three cases of attempted ⸱ ape. The first case of attempt was on a COLORED SCHOOL TEACHER. In three of these cases the suspect was one man and he was in jail when the riot started. Five weeks before the riot a WHITE MOTORMAN and a CONDUCTOR on a street car attempted RAPE upon TWO COLORED GIRLS who were the only passengers in the car when it reached the end of the line.

"The Washington Post, the paper most instrumental in fomenting the riot spirit in the nation's capital, in its issue of August 15, 1919, carried in a prominent place a 'story' (lie is better term) of a white woman being attacked by two young colored men at the carnival grounds, giving their description, etc. The following day, hidden on an inside page in an obscure place, this same organ of mob-violence and racial hate stated that the 'race story' was a fabrication and that the case had been dropped.

"In the Longview, Chicago, Knoxville and Elaine domestic disorders, not even the prejudiced and one-sided white press could assign RAPE as the casus belli. It was simply the hell-fired spirit to wreak out Hunnish 'kultur' by mobocratic exponents upon colored citizens and the unexpected happened: The black man stood his ground and fought in the same manner as he did for insuring democracy for his white brothers in Europe, Asia and the isles of the seas, as well as America.

"Despite the damage done at Omaha, until this good day no person has been found who could truthfully prove that the lynched black man had committed any rape. Really, the facts divulged show no case of rape.

"So much for that.

"What the record further shows: From 1883 to 1903, there were 1,985 colored Americans lynched in 'Bam.' Of that number rape was assigned as the cause in only 675 cases; other causes being given for the other 1,310 cases.

"In the past 30 years 50 COLORED WOMEN HAVE BEEN LYNCHED. In the past 18 months FIVE COLORED WOMEN HAVE BEEN LYNCHED. WERE THEY RAPISTS? IF SO WHO WERE THEIR VICTIMS? WERE THEY 'LECHEROUS BLACK BRUTES?' WERE THEIR ACTS OF RAPING CONDONED AND ABETTED BY THE COLORED RACE? One of the colored women lynched, Mrs. Mary Turner, Valdosta, Ga., despite the fact that she was eight months pregnant, was hanged head downwards, disemboweled and her unborn babe fell from her womb and was trampled upon by the Huns of America.

"In the five-year period, 1914-1918, exclusive of those murdered and butchered by the Turks of East St. Louis, 264 colored Americans were lynched in this boasted 'land of the free and home of the brave,' and out of this number rape was assigned as the cause in only 28 cases.

"Here is the lynching record of 1918 (colored) : Attacks on white women, 13; attacks on colored women, 1; living with white woman, 1; too revolting to publish, 2; shooting and killing officer of law, 10; murder of civilian, 14; shooting and wounding, 4; conspiracy to avenge killing of relative, 6; accomplice in murder, 3; aiding mob victim in attempt to escape, 1; intent to rob and kidnap, 1; quarrel with employer, 1; creating disturbance, 1; stealing hogs, 3; unknown, 2; total, 63; (whites) : disloyal utterances, 2; murder, 2; sum total 67.

"Thirteen of the colored victims of the American pastime and national sport were taken from the officers of the law or jails, many of whom had no trial. Take the Georgia case, where the mob lynched every colored man they saw, about five in number, and said that despite the fact that they had lynched the wrong man they would continue lynching the 'd—— niggers' until they got the right one. No alleged case of rape was the offense in the above case.

"During 1917 in New York County, which is only part of New York City, 230 persons were indicted for rape by the grand jury; 37 being indicted for rape in the first degree. In other words, the number of persons indicted in just a part of New York City for rape in the first degree exceeded by nine the total number of colored Americans lynched in the entire United States from 1914 to 1918. Among these 37 rapists indicted by the New York County grand jury, where the evidence must be convincing and conclusive (something that does not prevail where mob law reigns), there was NOT A SINGLE COLORED AMERICAN.

"The Informer challenges any man or paper to cite a single instance where a colored man in the South accused of rape upon a white woman has not been given a speedy trial and speedier execution. We also challenge any man or paper to cite one single instance where a white man has ever been arrested or indicted for criminal attacks upon colored women. Yet a glance at the different hues and shades in the colored race shows that somebody is mixing and messing things up very badly.

"The Informer deprecates any crime upon womanhood and favors the severest penalty for the offender; but it favors this through the orderly processes of law and order and respect for constituted authority.

"If the white man's civilization and system of jurisprudence can not mete out proper punishment to rapists and other offenders and violators of the law of society without resorting to mob violence and anarchy, then the proud and haughty Aryan civilization is a rank and dismal failure and should be consigned to the junk yard.

"Many of these alleged outrages charged to the colored race, while committed by BLACKENED MEN, are not always committed by BLACK MEN. Just a few weeks ago a heinous crime was committed in Vincennes, Ind., by the usual alleged 'big, black, burly brute.' Certain incriminating evidence gave the officers a clue and when the culprit was apprehended he was not even a member of the colored race.

"Scores of colored men have been lynched for crimes they never committed and knew absolutely nothing about. A colored printer, now in California, was barely saved from an angry and hungry mob in Palestine, Texas, a few years ago, for an alleged case of 'rape,' and when the facts became known and the identity of the real 'assailant' ascertained he was not a member of the colored race and there was no case of 'rape' in the strictest sense of the word.

"If the black man were a rapist and brute by nature and instinct, as these white newspapers, demagogues and mobocrats would have the public believe, why are so many black men employed in white homes as chauffeurs, butlers, yard men, etc.? Why are white women and children committed unto their care and keeping with such abandon by white men?

"Digressing for a moment: It is next to impossible for an unescorted, decent-looking colored woman to appear on the streets even in 'heavenly Houston' without being insulted and pursued by 'lecherous brutes' whose racial connection is not of Hamitic descent.

"The Informer does not deny that some foolish and ignorant colored men are guilty of the crime of rape, just like men of other races; but being the 'under-dog,' black fiends catch hell while other fiends go 'Scot-free.' Any alleged case of rape, where the perpetrator is of ebony-hue or reported to be of dark skin, is true, according to sentiment and custom; while on the other hand a rape committed by men of other races, even upon their own daughters, is always found a falsehood and the matter is invariably quashed.

"As long as white newspapers adroitly encourage mob-violence (as they are now doing) and play up alleged and reputed crimes committed by supposed colored men in glaring headlines, remarking that 'it is feared if the criminal is apprehended, he will be lynched;' as long as white statesmen (like Senator Williams of Mississippi), congressmen and ministers justify and condone lynch law for any crime; as long as moral cowardice is displayed by those in authority; as long as the states refuse to educate and symmetrically develop all their citizens; as long as America tolerates a double standard of citizenship and remains the world's most noteworthy hypocrite and sham; as long as white men co-habit with colored women and rear families by them; as long as he holds in bold defiance and utter contempt the laws he drafted and enacted solely and wholly—just that long will there be lynchings, riots and other internal upheavals.

"Our slogan must be: DOWN WITH MOBOCRACY! UP WITH DEMOCRACY! or it's hell to pay, Uncle Sam!"

1. *Number, Cause, Instances*

THE following report was printed throughout the colored press:

"75 Negroes Lynched—One a Woman, 7 Burned Alive, 9 Burned After Being Shot or Hanged, 19 Charged With Assault on Women

Tuskegee Institute, Ala., Dec. 31

"Dear Sir:

"I send you the following information relative to lynchings for the past year. According to the record compiled by Monroe N. Work, of the Department of Records and Research of the Tuskegee Institute, there were 82 lynchings in 1919, of which 77 were in the South and 5 in the North and West. This is 18 more than the number 64 for the year 1918. Of those lynched 75 were Negroes and 7 whites. One of those put to death was a Negro woman. Nineteen, or less than one-fourth of those put to death, were charged with rape or attempted rape. Seven of the victims were burned to death. Nine were put to death and then their bodies were burned. The charges against those burned to death were: rape, 3; murder, 2; killing sheriff, 1; no charge given, 1. The charges against those first killed and then their bodies burned were: attempted rape, 3; shooting officers of the law, 3; rape, 1; murder, 1; incendiary talk, 1.

"The offense of murder was charged against all the whites lynched. The offenses charged against the Negroes were: murder, 13; attempted rape, 10; rape, 9; abetting riots, 4; shooting officers of the law, 4; insulting a woman, 4; killing officer of the law, 4; alleged incendiary talk, 2; writing improper letter, 2; charge not reported, 6; shooting woman, 1; robbery, 1; murder sentence changed to life imprisonment, 1; shooting night watchman, 1; shooting and wounding a man, 1; alleged complicity in killing officer of the law, 1; killing man in self-defense, 1; killing landlord in dispute over crop settlement, 1; no charge made, 1; for being acquitted of shooting officer of the law, 1; remarks about Chicago race riot, 1; for keeping company with a white woman, 1; for being found under bed, 1; for making boastful remarks, 1; for alleged misleading of mobs searching for another, 1; because appeal was taken from ten years' sentence for attempting life of another, 1; for discussing a lynching, 1.

"The states in which lynchings occurred and the number in each state are as follows: Alabama, 7; Arkansas, 12; Colorado, 2; Florida, 5; Georgia, 21; Louisiana, 7; Mississippi, 12; Missouri, 2; Nebraska, 1; North Carolina, 3; South Carolina, 1; Tennessee, 1; Texas, 4; Washington, 1; West Virginia, 2; Kansas, 1.

"Very truly,
"ROBERT R. MOTON,
"Principal."
—*The Daily Herald* (Baltimore), January 2, 1920.

A few reports of lynchings will here be given as examples. While I accredit these items to the papers from which I clipped them the reader must understand that they appeared in practically the same form in hundreds of papers.

"Star City, Ark., June 20.—Clyde Ellison, who lived in this neighborhood, was lynched here last week when he refused to work for a white farmer. Ellison had been offered the sum of 85 cents a day to work in a cotton field. It was thought that he could be frightened into accepting the work, and a charge of assault on Miss Idelle Bennett (white), 18-year-old daughter of Dave Bennett, was placed against him. The girl, a characteristic type of backwoods ignorance, gave the plot away when she admitted that her father had told her of Ellison's refusal to work and of the part she was to play in the scheme to force him to pick cotton.

LYNCHERS GIVE WARNING

"A final appeal was made to Ellison, and following this he was seized, carried to a bridge and a rope tied around his neck. Flat irons were heated and placed upon his naked form and he was forced to jump off the structure. His neck was broken by the fall. His body was left hanging over night, and a sign reading: "This is how we treat lazy niggers," was tacked to his head. The sheriff and deputies were notified to come and cut the body down.

FARMS DESERTED

"Every one who took part in the lynching is known here, as the town is so small that people could be recognized by their voices, let alone their faces. Since this crime all of Bennett's farm labor has left him and the farms in the surrounding country are deserted."—*The Colorado Statesman* (Denver), July 5.

"COLORED WOMAN BEATEN BY CALIFORNIA MOB

Courts to Act to Avoid Trouble

Oakland, Cal., Aug. 21.—What is easily described as one of the most primitive, brutal and cowardly crimes in a supposed civilized community was the cowardly attack by white hoodlums upon Mr. William Harris, wife and daughter, who reside at 617 Jackson street, a so-called exclusive residential section of Oakland, Cal.

HARRIS WEALTHY CITIZEN

"Mr. Harris is one of the wealthiest colored men in this section of the country. He owns valuable real estate in the heart of the city. His daughter is a student at the University of California and is said to be one of the most popular and brilliant matriculants.

MOB ATTACKS TWICE

"The mob, it is said, made first an attack upon Mr. Harris, who was not reluctant about defending himself and his home. Their efforts to frighten Mr. Harris proving a failure, the savages feared to return in person. With the financial aid of certain white real estate sharks, it is alleged they hired some of the lower element of white women to attack Mrs. and Miss Harris.

WOMEN BEATEN

"In making a complaint in his request for a warrant, Mr. Harris stated that these women, without ceremony or provocation, came to his home, called his wife and daughter to the door and by a preponderance of numbers succeeded in giving them a severe beating. If the courts fail to prosecute the offenders it is reported that serious trouble will follow."—*The Whip* (Chicago).

"Colored Soldier Shot to Death by Arkansas Mob

Pine Bluff, Ark., Sept. 13.—Flinton Briggs, a discharged Negro soldier, just returned from overseas, was shot and killed by a mob three miles south of Star City, Ark., Monday afternoon.

"According to reports, Briggs was walking along the sidewalk, when he met a white couple, and as he stepped to one side to let them pass, the white woman brushed into him and said, 'Niggers get off of the sidewalk down here.' Briggs replied, that this was a free country. No sooner than he had made the remarks, the woman's escort seized him. As he tussled to get away from his opponent, other whites going along the street quickly ganged around. Briggs was quickly thrust into a passing automobile and was taken about two or three miles out from town, followed by three or four car loads of white hoodlums.

"After the hoodlums had reached the edge of town, they found they could not secure a rope to lynch the innocent soldier with, so they took automobile chains and chained him to a tree, after which he was made the target of forty or fifty rifle and revolver bullets.

"Briggs' body was found by a farmer, who reported it to the authorities. The coroner, who held an inquest over the body, gave verdict that he had come to his death by a mob of unknown persons. Up to the present writing nothing has been done to try to find a clue or no investigations have been started.

"Many colored farmers, who live around in the vicinity have voiced their intentions of leaving, and many have already left for the North."—*The Whip* (Chicago).

"CHARRED BODY OF A COLORED MAN FOUND IN CHURCH DEBRIS

Edifice Believed to Have Been Fired by Incendiaries in Laurens County, Georgia

Eastman, Ga., Aug. 28.—The charred body of Eli Cooper, an aged Laurens County Negro, who resided two miles from

Caldwell was found to-day in ashes of Petway's Gift Church which was burned by incendiaries at an early hour this morning. Three other Negro churches and a Negro lodge near Caldwell were burned on Tuesday night.

"Cooper is alleged to have been talking considerably of late in a manner offensive to the white people. It is alleged that a Chicago Negro newspaper that had been circulated among the Negroes here for several days has caused unrest among them.

"The white residents were informed that an uprising of Negroes was set for thirty days from yesterday. Cooper's own remarks it is alleged, were to the effect that the Negroes had been 'run over for fifty years, but this will all change in thirty days.'

．　　．　　．　　．　　．　　．　　．

"Cooper was taken from his home Wednesday night, according to a story told by his wife, by a crowd of fifteen or twenty white men.

"The church was discovered in flames at 1 o'clock this morning. Shortly before the fire was discovered residents of the neighborhood were aroused by shooting, about fifty shots having been fired."—*The Planet* (Richmond), September 6.

In September, long before the Phillips County affair, the following item was printed by all the colored press:

"FIFTH LYNCHING IN ARKANSAS

Sheriff Takes Man's Heart Home as a Souvenir —Body Tied to an Automobile and Dragged Through the Principal Streets

Bogalusa, La.—(Special)—Instead of the white people celebrating Labor Day here as they do in the Northern states, with parades and address and showing to the world that the Southern white man is not a savage, they celebrated it by putting a rope around the neck of Lucias McCarty, a young man who had rendered excellent service for his country in France, and dragged his body around the principal streets tied to an automobile. Over 5,000 took part in the killing. After being

Lynchings 105

dragged for over an hour his body was then saturated with kerosene and piles of wood laid on him and then burned to a crisp. He was accused of insulting a white woman. "The newspapers had been advertising the burning for several days. The town was overrun with crackers to witness the burning."—*The Guardian* (Boston), September 13.

Two other typical reports of lynchings will suggest how a news item may be more potent than an editorial:

"WHIPS COLORED WOMAN FOR ASK-ING ABOUT $1.50

Mississippi Mob Called Out Husband, Whipped Wife

"What took place in Laurel, Miss., Aug. 20, 1919, while Colored people were conducting a meeting there.

"A colored woman had taken a lady's wash home and received $1.50 pay; on return, she got a letter out of the P. O. opened it and read it, then put the $1.50 in the envelope with the letter and up the street she lost the envelope and the contents. There were some white boys playing near the spot where she jumped a small stream. She missed the envelope and returned in search for it. She asked the boys if they had seen it. They said 'No,' and turned their pockets to show, except one boy who ran to the house. As she went to ask the lady of the house to have him give her the envelope, she was given rough words.

"That night, a crowd of whites went to her home, commanded her husband to come out. They took her out about 3 or 4 blocks and whipped her, and gave her the letter and $0.50 of the money and brought her back to the house. It was told that none of the men were masked."—*The Guardian* (Boston), September 13.

"Yazoo City Man Whipped By Mob

Jackson, Miss., Oct. 2.—Drummond Leonard, a prominent, and said to be a wealthy Colored man, who was born and reared in Yazoo City, Miss., was taken from a train in Annie,

Mississippi, by seven Jackson white men and hurried off to the swamps where it is feared he was lynched. Leonard had brought his son and two daughters to Jackson and placed them on a train for Atlanta, Ga., where they were going to attend school. Reports that come from Yazoo City, said that there had been a conspiracy against Leonard's life for some time, from the fact that he operated a barber shop in Yazoo City, Miss., and was well patronized by the best white people of the town. Threats for the last past year had been made against Leonard's life, but his reputation was such among the better class of white men that they advised him not to leave, saying that he would have ample protection. All indications point to jealousy and conspiracy. Thousands of Negroes are reported to be getting ready to leave the state of Mississippi on account of the mob's action."—*The Times Plain Dealer* (Birmingham, Ala.), October 4.

"A Brutal Assault on an Aged Minister

Palatka, Fla., Oct. 4.—A brutal and cowardly assault was made on the Rev. F. M. Spicer, a retired minister of the Florida Conference of the Methodist Episcopal Church, on Tuesday morning, September 30, as he was returning from Crescent City, where he had been assisting Rev. A. Lee in a revival meeting. A mob had gathered in the city during the night, supposedly of people outside of the city, to lynch the Negro who shot and killed the conductor on the previous Sunday morning. When Rev. Spicer stepped from the north bound train, which arrives at the depot at about 4:20 A. M., a ruffian struck him a terrific blow on the side of the head. Before he realized what was going on another one struck him supposedly with the butt of the gun, which felled him to the ground. In a moment a half dozen or more guns were pointed on him while he was lying on the ground, and the crowd began to kick him, and otherwise brutally assaulted him, until some one from the crowd asked the men to stop beating the old man, after he had pleaded piteously for his life. They left him in a serious condition, which at one time was thought to be fatal. But by the close attention of Dr. White, he is gradually recovering. The citizens of Palatka, of both races, were greatly incensed over the brutal attack on this innocent and harmless minister of the gospel.

"Rev. Spicer is highly respected by all who know him, and all

alike regret the occurrence. Several other persons were assaulted also, but none so shamefully as was Rev. Spicer. The
city counsel, the mayor, the sheriff and other officials of both
county and city strongly condemned the outrage, and promised
full protection to the colored citizens at whatever cost. This
is one of the most peaceful cities in the State. The whites
and the colored folks seem to understand each other, and the
most peaceful relation exists between them."—*The Commonwealth* (Baltimore), October 29.

"NEGRO KILLED IN HOSPITAL"

Killed While Confined to Bed by Wounds

Montgomery, Ala., Oct. 9.—John Temple, Negro, who last
night shot and fatally wounded Policeman John Barbare and
who was wounded by the officer, was shot to death in a hospital early to-day by a small band of white men.

"He was the third Negro to die by lynch law within a period
of twelve hours, Miles Phifer and Robert Crosky, the latter a
discharged soldier, having been shot to death by a mob five
miles from the city yesterday afternoon. Still another Negro,
Bird Astor, who was with Temple when Barbare who was shot,
was being sought by a posse and it was believed his capture
would result in more mob violence.

"A fourth Negro, Ben Miller, a former soldier, was shot and
wounded early to-day on a downtown street. He reported
four white men had attempted to get him into an automobile,
and he was shot when he refused to go with them."—*The
Dallas Express,* October 11.

"FORMER COLORED SOLDIER LYNCH-ED FOR HAVING WHITE SWEETHEART

Leading Citizens Are Silent on Disgraceful Affair

Clarksdale, Miss.—Although L. B. Reed, formerly a soldier
in the American Expeditionary Forces, was lynched here on
September 10, the officers of the law, as usual, are criminally
indifferent and making no attempt to punish the guilty parties.

"The ex-Colored soldier was taken from the Mosby Hotel
and strung up from the bridge across the Sunflower River.

The body was found in the water three days later and buried the following day.

"Reed was put to death for showing marked attention to a white woman who stopped at the Mosby Hotel, but who took her meals at the Clarksdale Café, where the dead man was employed as a waiter. It is charged that a Colored bellboy informed the lynchers of the intimacy existing between Reed and the white woman.

"If white men were to be lynched for insulting and seeking to thrust their attentions on colored women here there would be lynchings daily.—*The Louisville News,* October 18.

The Birmingham Times Plain Dealer of October 11 contained on its front page the following six items:

"SHERIFF FLEES WITH NEGRO, BUT IS CAUGHT

Lincolnton, Ga., Oct: 6.—Jack Gordon and Will Brown, Negroes, were lynched by a mob here early to-day and their bodies burned." [Details.]

"Georgia Mob Takes Negro from Sheriff and Riddles Body With Bullets

Macon, Ga., Oct. 8.—Special to The Plain Dealer.—Eugene Hamilton, a Negro, under 10-year sentence for an attempt on the life of Charles Tingle, Jasper county farmer, was taken from Sheriff Middlebrooks of Jones county, near here early to-day, and shot to death at daylight near Monticello, in Jasper county." [Details.]

"Negro Taken to Mobile

Montgomery, Ala., Oct. 6.—Fearing mob violence, acting Chief of Police W. J. Leavell Sunday night spirited James Cox, Jr., Negro, away from the city jail to a place of safety, presumably the state penitentiary at Wetumpka, following his arrest on a charge of disorderly conduct, in committing an insult in the presence of a young white woman." [Details.]

"Folks Leaving Montgomery

Montgomery, Ala., Oct. 9.—Special to The Times Plain Dealer.—The recent lynching of three Negroes here has caused an unrest among our people and they are leaving in large numbers. So many of the leading Negroes of the city are preparing to leave as soon as they can possibly get their affairs settled." [Details.]

"Mob Rushes Jail but Prisoner is Gone

Huntington, W. Va., Oct. 7.—Three hundred men rushed the jail here last night in a search for a Georgia Negro, giving the name of B. Anderson. He is charged with assaulting a white woman." [Details.]

"Two Negroes Are Burned, One Shot

Washington, Ga., Oct. 6.—Special to The Times Plain Dealer.—Two Negroes burned at the stake, another shot to death and several whipped, was the toll exacted by mobs in Lincoln county yesterday and early this morning for the shooting of Deputy Red Freeman and a citizen who attempted to assist him in arresting Jack Gordon, a Negro, on a minor charge.

"Jack Gordon, Freeman's assailant, and Will Brown were burned near Lincolnton to-day. Brown was charged with aiding Gordon in escaping after he had shot Freeman. The third Negro to lose his life, Moses Freeman, was killed yesterday because he attempted to throw the pursuers off Gordon's trail." [Details.]

In the four corners of the front page of *The Houston Informer,* November 8, were the four following news items, printed in heavy black type with large headlines:

"Colored Youth is Given Dose of South's Democratic Kultur; Burned to Death, Says Report

"Special to The Informer.

"Crosby, Tex., Nov. 5, 1919.—One of the most Hunnish

and heathenish cruelties ever perpetrated in a civilized country
was staged here on October 27. Several colored men were
working for a rice farmer and they were brought to town to
be paid off.

"One colored boy was brought to Crosby, presumably to be
paid off, when a mob took him out of the car, poured three
gallons of gasoline on him and after throwing him in the cala-
boose, threw matches on him and set him on fire, burning him
into ashes.

"Details of the alleged crime and the personnel of the mob
have not been ascertained, but the daily white newspapers
have been 'mum' about this atrocity, which happened almost
in a stone's throw of Harris County court house."

"Secretary Newton D. Baker Dismissed White Male Clerk for Insulting Colored Female

"Special to The Informer.

"Washington, D. C.—Mrs. Ida Dorsey, colored, employed in
the adjutant general's office of the war department, was insulted by a white clerk, who indecently and wilfully exposed
himself to her. Mrs. Dorsey called for assistance. The would-
be assailant was placed under arrest and then released. The
matter was later brought to the attention of Secretary of War
Baker, who summarily dismissed the clerk."

"White Postmaster Ran Amuck at Liberty, Beating Race Woman Into State of Insensibility,

"Special to The Informer.

"Liberty, Texas, Nov. 5. 1919.—A colored woman of about
38 years of age was beaten almost to death with a club
here by the postmaster and her clothes torn from her body,
because she asked the second time for a letter that she had
a right to believe was in the postoffice for her.

"It appears that the letter had been there about a week
or ten days and when she went to the United States postoffice
(mind you) and asked for it a second time, this chivalrous (?)
and gallant (?) postmaster remarked: 'Not only will I keep
your letter, but I will beat you to death,' and only divine
providence prevented him from carrying out his threat."

"Dayton Merchant Beat Race Woman with Ax Handle Because She Desired to Exchange Shoes

"Special to The Informer.

"Dayton, Texas, Nov. 5, 1919.—One of our colored women was brutally and inhumanely beaten with an ax handle here October 28. She had purchased a pair of child's shoes from the Dayton Mercantile Company the preceding day and carried them back to be exchanged.

"When she insisted upon exchanging the shoes, this progressive and manly (?) merchant cursed her, jumped over the counter, grabbed an ax handle and pursued her two blocks down the streets, striking her terrible blows with the handle every step of the way and no one asked him to desist in his brutality and barbarism."

Occupying the upper center of the page were the following headlines in heavy type:

"PROSPEROUS LOUISIANA COLORED CITIZENS FORCED TO MIGRATE TO MORE CIVILIZED CLIMES; MOB SPIRIT ON RAMPAGE IN SOUTHERN STATES"

Across the full top of the page were headlines proclaiming these several crimes. Could anything add to the effectiveness of this exhibit? Yes, one thing, and that, of course, was not overlooked. This poem was placed in the lower center of the page:

"He Sleeps in France's Bosom

(A Tribute to Our Fallen Black Braves Over There.)

"He sleeps in France's bosom,
The brave, of yesterday;
Who gave his life while fighting
To save Democracy.

"He fell a gallant patriot,
    Amidst the hot affray:
'Neath stars and stripes, o'er waving,
    Upon the cold, cold clay.

"No one was there to help him,
    No mother's voice was near
To say, 'Rise up, my darling,
    I'm here, so do not fear.'

"No sister's lip did kiss him,
    No wife did hold his head;
Alone, midst foes and strangers,
    America's son fell dead.

"But hush! Here comes a message,
    From far across the sea;
In crimson red 'tis written:
    'I gave my life for thee.

" 'My life, I freely gave it,
    For you and liberty;
'Tis all I had to offer,
    My peaceful fair country.

" 'Tell mother dear, don't worry,
    Her son is now at rest.
He sleeps 'mong France's fairest,
    As one of America's best.'

"He sleeps in France's bosom,
    In No Man's Land, somewhere;
To wake no more, till Gabriel
    Calls him to mansions fair."
                    —*Rev. H. D. Greene.*

In the same columns with these reports of lynchings are
to be found such news items as the following. These two
classes of news have a clear relation to each other:

"HATED IN DAY TIME LOVED AT NIGHT

Tennessee Cracker Has Dual Character. Is Both Negro Hater and Keeper of Colored Mistresses

Knoxville, Tenn., October, 23.—A real Dr. Jekyll and Mr. Hyde is George W. Howard, white, of Fort Worth, Texas, who was here on a visit last week. During the day-time, Howard is the kind of Southern cracker, who moves in the best society, and is handy with the gun and ripe to keep colored folks in their place. At night he makes his way to the home of some colored paramour and lingers until the next morning.

"Here is a part of Howard's story as reported in the East Tennessee News: 'I arrived in Knoxville to visit relatives Thursday, and about noon, thot I'd set out to hunt me up a little "nigger gal." I came to the house down where they live and saw that little black one over there (pointing to 16-year-old Mattie Lee) and I spoke to her and walked in her house. I wasn't there long until that one (pointing to Fannie Mae Henderson) crawled out from under the bed. A little later that one (referring to the third of the trio, Sallie Watkins) came in and we started to playing. The girls got so rough that I asked them to stop until I put on my clothes. I finally got on my clothes, gave the little "gal" a dollar, and offered to pay her for a curtain I had torn down. It was then I discovered that my "wad of greenbacks" amounting to $437.00 was gone.'

"The girls were held for court under $3,000 bond."—*The Associated Negro Press.*

"McRae is in Telfair County, Ga. Several young white gentlemen (?) invaded the Negro quarters and sought to force their attentions upon two Colored girls. The girls ran from them to the protection of an aged Colored man, 72 years of age. In the attack which followed, this old man, defending his own life and the honor of his two girls, killed one of the white 'gentlemen,' and gave himself up to the authorities. A mob of ten persons then overpowered (?) the county authorities and lynched the old man. The good (?) citizens of the county, deploring the act, pledged themselves to conceal the facts from the outside world."—*The Wisconsin Weekly Blade* (Madison), August 28.

"Two young (white) Milwaukeeans, returned soldiers, are awaiting trial for a criminal assault on two young girls, which the newspapers call the 'most atrocious in local history.' Still no one has ventured to call them 'white brutes.' "—*Ibid*, October 9.

Of the many editorial denunciations that have been poured out unceasingly, in terms the most vigorous the English language could furnish, I must make choice of but a few, as usual.

"Sham, Just Sham!

With newspapers giving advance notices of the intention to lynch and burn, southern communities are put in an unenviable position.   But with officials saying they are powerless, and surrendering their sworn duty for fear armed resistance to mob violence might mean bloodshed, as did Gov. Bilbo of Mississippi, civilization trembles.   The American people felt a righteous wrath over the sinking of the Lusitania, but a hundred Lusitanias are not worth the whole fabric of law which man has evolved out of his struggles upward.   Sheer hypocrisy to talk of humanity or brotherhood while Mississippi or any other lyncher's paradise is part of the Union."—*The Kansas City* [Mo.] *Call*, July 9.

"THEORY VS. PRACTICE

·   ·   ·   ·   ·   ·   ·

There is no ground deep enough to bury the memory of an epoch, nation, community or individual who, professing the creed of Christ, vilifies, misrepresents, burns, lynches, assaults and crushes both the body and soul of a people, loyal thrifty and brave.

"Human torches have lighted the faces of fiends only in ancient barbaric Rome and modern cultured America.

"The hour is, indeed, at hand to abandon the policy of former slave-holders or earn the united condemnation of all future unbiased writers of history."—*The Washington Eagle*, September 13.

"?

Montgomery, Ala., Oct. 3.—The special grand jury organized at the call of Judge Leon McCord, of the Montgomery
county circuit court, which began its duties Thursday at noon
investigating the lynchings of Robert Crosby Relium Phifer
and William Temple, Negroes, here Monday afternoon and
night, reported to Judge McCord this morning that they were
unable to secure any information leading to the identity of any
member of the two mobs and asked to be discharged, which was
granted."—*The East Tennessee News* (Knoxville), October 9.

"Georgia's Blood-Curdling Deed

Was there ever a more shocking, disgraceful scene upon this
American continent—this land of the free and home of the
brave—than that which occurred in old bloodstained heathen
Georgia last week, when sixty-five 'good white men,' proud,
civilized, and intelligent white men, lynched Eugene Hamilton, already convicted of assault and attempt to murder? This
blood-curdling dastardly savage deed is almost too brutal to
print.

. . . .

"If white America really stands for liberty (and this is what
our President and Government have preached and still
preach) it must hold out to every citizen, regardless of color,
creed or previous condition of servitude, the scepter of true
democracy, backed by the law of this government. If liberty
is sacred (and this is what the white people preached to the
world, to justify America's entrance into the war against
Germany) law is also sacred. The Constitution of these United
States provides for but one king in America, and that is the
law, and no republic or government can continue to stand
upon such constant and increasing disregard of its only king.
"White men make the law, white men execute the law, white
men keep all of the jails, then, why should there ever be any
need of them lynching a Negro if guilty of any sort of crime?
This Negro boy had been arrested, tried and convicted in the
courts of Georgia, by Georgia white men and was still in the
hands of Georgia white men for safe keeping—why should

other Georgia white men lynch him, except to vent that savage bloodthirsty nature which seems to be a part of the white race?

"American white men, governors, senators, representatives, judges, statesmen and political leaders are braying like thirsty jack-asses, frothing at the mouth and railing upon Mexico for her reported atrocities against American citizens, and wanting this government to order an intervention to stop what these white American proselytes of rebel democracy call 'savagery.' But, can white America successfully do this, without first 'clearing her own conscience?'

"We can't bring ourselves to believe that the soil of Russia, China, or Mexico, has ever been marked with such barbarous crimes as these perpetrated in old hell-charged heathen Georgia and half-civilized America."—*The Galveston New Idea,* October 25.

On the spread of lynching in "the Benighted States" (Afro-American for United States) the following is a brief résumé:

"Mob Law Rampant

A Nebraska city added to list of lynch-law-abiding communities.

"It's growing like a pestilence; it spreads like forest fires; it breaks out here, there, God knows where next.

"A filthy, hideous, terrible thing, it is engulfing our country down its great, red maw.

"For years it seemed chained to the unregenerate South. It stalked boldly in Georgia. Waxed mighty in Texas and Florida. It still is lord supreme in the land of the cotton and the corn.

"In the boldness of its hellish might, it invaded the Capital of the Nation. The hallowed precincts, over which the cenotaph of Washington looks down, where Lincoln signed the Emancipation Proclamation, where the immortal Roosevelt dealt rugged justice with a tender hand of mercy, become teeming and vocal with the awful bigness of the Beast, yelping as he scents the kill. Chicago, Knoxville, Charleston, New York City next fall before the monstrous onrush."—*The Searchlight* (Seattle, Wash.), October 4.

2. The Negro and the Crime of Rape

"Negroes Do Not Condone Crime

It has been stated, especially by Southerns, that Negro leaders and those who have endeavored to help the Negro's cause in America so that right and justice may be his portion along with the other groups of citizens do not devote enough of their time and efforts in condemning and preventing crime among Negroes, and this charge against the leaders and friends of our race is based on a false assumption prompted by race prejudice.

"If there is any person or persons in the United States who think or assume that the Negro is so instinctively criminal that it is necessary for the leaders of the race to form organizations throughout the country to teach him to obey the laws of the land, they are badly mistaken.

"We, the leaders among our race, and those who have helped our cause do not condone crime committed by white or black, and we naturally hate to hear of a crime committed by those whom we are trying to help, but we do not see why the crimes of one class should be magnified and the other class considered as a matter of course.

"We deny that the Negro is any more a criminal than any other class or group which make up the people of this country. All we ask is a fair trial. We do not hide or attempt to ˙hide the criminals among us. All we ask is equal justice before the law.

"A prosecuting officer of St. Louis said: 'Not half of the colored men and youths who are sentenced would be convicted if they were properly represented before the courts of this city.' If that is the case in St. Louis, God help the colored men, women and children who come before the courts of the South. This accounts for the penal institutions of the land being the abiding place for so many of our race.

"We are fighting crime wherever we see it; we are fighting lawlessness wherever it seeks to trample the law under its feet, just as every good, true and loyal American citizen should do. Yet we feel that we are peculiarly interested in these things because it is the members of our race who are victims of crime and lawlessness.

"We have been sinned against more than we have sinned."—
The St. Louis Argus, October 10.

"Congressman J. T. Heflin claims that the crime of rape started the race riots recently in Washington with the colored man as the perpetrator of the outrage. This distinguished southerner knows better than this. Did rape start the East St. Louis massacres? Did rape start the riot in Philadelphia? Did rape start the trouble in Chicago? The cause is racial antipathy on the part of chronic white disturbers, who envy the progress of respectable colored people and who use every means to discredit and injure them.

"A black rapist is no worse than a white rapist. Why not the black and the white people unite to rid the communities of both classes of this kind of people? The excuses amount to nothing. The better class of white people and the better class of colored people understand each other. Let this class coöperate in bettering conditions and in eliminating an evil that is generally recognized. There is not a black crook in the United States to-day, who did not receive his instructions from a white crook.

"The lower element of black people believe in the white man of the underworld and will generally do what he tells them to do. When it comes to devilish ingenuity and scandalous crimes, we find that we have much of this kind of material thrown over into our 'back yards' by white people, who have trained them in crime and who have educated them in all of the sleight of hand performances of dishonesty. On the other hand thousands of white people, who wish us well have been educating us and helping up along the lines of upright living."—*The Planet* (Richmond), August 16.

"The White Man Who Knows the Negro

The greatest ignorance evinced by any white man or woman is that which is shown by the white person who claims that he knows the Negro. 'I know the Negro,' he begins, and all that follows is a demonstration of how little he really knows about the subject. 'I have slept with the Negro, played with the Negro, and eaten with the Negro, and I had an old Black Mammy,' he continues, 'and the biggest trouble with the colored people is that there are so many bad ones among them. These bad ones spoil the work of the good ones.' This old trite expression from white people is either down-right lying or ignorance. This is merely the Hell-born propaganda that our enemies have used in order to discredit the entire race. Many well-meaning Southern white people, like a nest of naked birds, have, all these years, lifted their thoughtless heads to swallow down whatever was poked into their mouths, if that 'whatever' was something against the Negro. How many bad ones are among the whites? Do their bad ones do away with the good works of their good ones? If not, why should Negroes be thought of in that way? No. It is a propaganda lie, and they know it. The goodness of the Negro that guarded white womanhood before and during the Civil War, the loyalty and service of the Negro in the war just ended—the meekness and humility of the race—these are the good things that give the race a place and promise in America. It would be a poor inducement to any people to think that they are to be forever rated by their 'bad ones.' The sun has 'dark spots' upon it but its chief characteristics are heat and light. Any white man who claims to know the Negro should know that he speaks the vilest untruth when he claims that the so many bad ones among us completely neutralized our good works. Let no one again think nor speak this old superannuated falsehood."—*The People's Pilot* (Richmond), August.

"Race Willingness to Coöperate Worthy of the Nation's Attention

There is a certain attitude of the Race so generally prevalent that it should challenge national attention in these days of widespread estrangement of classes and groups. There is, everywhere, a willingness of the Race to coöperate with other Americans for the purpose of a better understanding between Blacks and Whites.

"While Labor and Capital struggle and commissions try almost vainly to bring them together, Black Americans take the initiative and ask for conferences that will enable the races to know each other better. While the Government contends with Bolsheviki among many of the Caucasian groups, Race leaders and organizations counsel respect for law, loyalty to the Government, and plead for official coöperation in allaying race friction. Extending the hand of brotherhood always, putting forth the arm of defense only when attacked, Black Americans are everywhere urging get-together meetings, careful study of conditions, remedies for friction. From the South, from the North, comes the same appeal. The West shows the same attitude. Is it not significant that the most proscribed and assailed group of Americans is at this time the most insistent for opportunity to coöperate with other Americans for America's good?

"The Negro was once accused of shielding his criminals. This he disproved. Much has been said of the necessity for coöperation between the better elements of both races. Particularly is this the sentiment in times of difficulty. But the Race is now ready, as it has always been, and insisting that these better elements of both race groups in the nation must come together, consult, advise, and coöperate in normal times. In fact, the Race is thus taking the only sensible position for the welfare of all America.

"This attitude of Black Americans is one of the most significant features in national life to-day. This outspoken desire to treat, to reach an understanding, should be met by the Government, by authorities in the State and city. The Race is ready to state its program, to suggest what it can do and to learn what it is desired it should do as its part in allaying strife and bringing about coöperation for the realization of true American ideals.

"Plainly then, that group of Americans which is said to create the 'Race Problem' is willing to do its full part to bring an end to the so-called Race Problem by helping to reduce it to terms of an American problem which can then be solved by application of the accepted rules for general American problems.

"The plea of the world is for coöperation to displace antagonism. It is not saying too much to assert that America's future depends upon the success with which she can obtain the coöperation of the various classes and groups of the nation.

"Shall not the spirit of coöperation evinced by Black America and by an element of White America also, be encouraged? Shall it not be sincerely met by authority, by all of White America?"—*The New Age* (Los Angeles), September 12.

3. *The White Man and the Crime of Rape*

" 'Attacks On White Women'

·   ·   ·   ·   ·   ·   ·ı

IT IS THE SAME OLD EXCUSE—'attacks on white women.' What the nature of these attacks have been is left to inference. Singularly nearly all race disturbances of this nature have this same stock excuse. If some Negro miscreant snatches the purse of a white woman, or some member of our group jostles some white woman upon the street, the cry is immediately raised that an attack has been made on a white woman. No effort is made to bring out the true facts, but the public is left to believe another sort of crime has been committed. The word 'attack' is deliberately confused wherever Colored and white are concerned. If the press of the country were honest in their statements concerning such matters race rioting would be robbed of its chief inspiration.

"IF THE MEN of our group were to make reprisals upon the white people for the wrongs done the women of our race, America would see a red day. During the period of slavery the lecherous white master consorted with the slave women of his plantation and filled the South with his tawny offspring. The white sons of this master class are to-day passing laws to segregate their yellow kinsmen, but, if all reports are true, the separatist measures are only intended for daylight.

"IF WE WERE TO RAISE the same barrier against them that they raise against us, what an outcry there would be! No doubt there will always be more or less friction between the white and Colored people in this country, but the white man ought to at least be consistent. If he does not like us that is his privilege, but he should find a better excuse for the injustice and wrongs perpetrated upon us than the one which prompts him to shield his evil doings behind the skirts of his women."—*The Chicago Defender*, September 20.

"The charge against white criminals of employing burnt cork to blacken themselves and to be mistaken for Negroes is common. One out of many: A recent case is that of Luther Wilson, a white man of Lacooche, Florida, charged with attempted criminal assault upon a white relative by marriage while she was on her way to school. Wilson, who had blacked his face, was recognized by the girl. He escaped after having been arrested, and shot Deputy Sheriff B. C. Wilcox of Sorrent."—*The Charleston* [S. C.] *Messenger*, August 9.

The two following items are placed here, though they are not cases of rape, because they are instances of the use of burnt cork:

"Disguised as 'Dark Man' to Lash Another Woman

Asheville, N. C., Sept. 12.—The 'Negro man' who horse-whipped Mrs. Wm. Crisp (white) thus adding oil to the fire of race hatred in this section, was neither a 'Negro nor a man,' but a white woman who disguised herself.

"This fact was brought out by officers who said they had obtained a confession from Mrs. Josephine Moody (white), wife of a prominent lawyer, that it was she who had horse-whipped Mrs. Crisp. A Defender reporter learned that the confession was obtained only after a threat had been made to put bloodhounds on the trail. The news of the attack so enraged the whites of the community that serious trouble was expected every minute. This was due to the fact that the white newspapers had declared that a 'Negro man' was the woman's assailant"—*The Chicago Defender*, September 13

"We see that at South Carrollton, Ky., three white men disguised as Negroes by blacking their faces, held up the cashier of the Citizens' Bank there recently and escaped with $23,000 in government bonds and $8,000 in currency, after wounding City Marshal Mack Ashby."—*The Charleston* [S. C.] *Messenger*, September 20.

"Pass It Along

· · · · · · ·

"No crime committed by Negroes can be laid at the door of the white man but the white man can black up and does, and often heaps upon the Negro a crime record and therefore by the record increases the percentage of crime among Negroes. There is no way of proving the percentage of this burnt cork criminal class but it is sufficiently large to affect the situation as a whole.

"One of the most sensational happenings in the South in recent years took place in Holly Springs, Mississippi, when a white man who was infatuated with a colored girl sought to prevent a colored man from calling upon this colored girl. This white man blackened up his face, went to the home of the colored girl and shot both the girl and her visitor. He attempted to get back home; a fire broke out in the town in the meantime and the man was caught, with his face blackened. He came from one of the prominent families.

"Not every Negro is as black as he is painted to be, nor is every white man as white as he claims to be."—*The Southwestern Christian Advocate* (New Orleans), September 11.

On "the hell-holes in Galveston's redlight district" *The Galveston New Idea,* October 25, thus concludes an editorial:

"IT IS DEPLORABLE and much regretted that the strong arm of the law, both of the City and County, is unable to cope with this wretched situation. It is a known fact, that many of these Colored women cohabit with white men—some live outright with white men, under disguise of being the white man's 'housekeeper.' Is there not a remedy for this? Would not the law, backed by the entire white citizenship, stop a white woman from living in a house with a Colored man as 'housekeeper?' There are no houses in this district occupied by white women, that could exist, if they were known to admit Colored men.

"DECENT COLORED GALVESTON will heartily endorse a drastic crusade against this corrupt condition to the end, that this part of Galveston especially, and other parts in general, will cease to be dens for the moral destruction of Colored girls and women."

"ANOTHER KU-KLUX KLAN FORMED

New Organization Will Keep White Men Away From Colored Women

Birmingham, Ala., Oct. 23.—Proposing the formation of the Secret Fraternal and Benevolent Order as the best means of helping to keep the white blood pure and of preventing any improper 'social equality' between white and colored races, a new organization has taken its place among the many clubs and societies in the south.

"Unlike the Ku-Klux Klan, its object of attack is not the Negro rapist, but white men who believe in social equality after dark.

"This Order has been incorporated by some pioneer spirits mainly of Marion, Alabama, and their program is to push it as effective propaganda to race purity. It contemplates rigid enforcement of laws against all forms of miscegenation, and would begin with the education of young white boys who would be graduated into an older order.

"White men who bridge the race line will be regarded by the new organization as 'traitors' to the white race.

"A real Dr. Jekyll and Mr. Hyde is increasing in alarming numbers."—*The Afro-American* (Baltimore). October 24.

"The Crimson Stain

SOME imaginative, dramatic novelists and scientists have seen fit to describe the presence of one-sixteenth or more Negro blood within one's veins as the crimson stain.

"In the United States to-day there are over 1,000,000 mulattoes, octoroons and quadroons, that are so Caucasian in appearance that science is baffled, civilization is double-crossed, and yet America seems asleep. Ninety-five per cent of these hybrid people have gone over on the other side. They look like white people; they talk like white people. They work in white men's jobs. They associate with white people; they marry white women, but they always think as Negroes. THE AMERICAN NEGRO HAS AN ENTIRELY DIFFERENT PSYCHOLOGY FROM THAT OF THE WHITE MAN. Conditions force it upon him. He is not allowed to think as an American, but as an American Negro. THE STIGMATIZED MIND OF THE AMERICAN NEGRO IS THE REAL CURSE OF AMERICAN PREJUDICE. That the mind of the ex-colored man always remains colored is admitted by all who follow the color line, the fear of his ultimate disclosure, the fear of fate's hands on his children, who sometimes are Negroid, the love for his old playmates and associates, the memory of the old insults and indignities and the knowledge that his fellows are still suffering, keeps his mind forever colored and the spark of loyalty for his colored progenitors from ever dying.

"THERE IS ANOTHER TYPE OF MULATTOES THAT LEAD HYDE AND JEKYLL EXISTENCES; TO-DAY WHITE, TO-MORROW BLACK. These individuals with uncanny instincts always seem to find out the sinister intrigue of the white man and forewarns and therefore remains the Negro. The activities of the Kenwood and Hyde Park Associations, and the plans of the white rioters were exposed through these Jekylls and Hydes. America's eyes are closed. They need no fears of social equality or Negro domination. The real fear is the crimson stain.

"Many who sit in high places are stained. It is claimed that three senators now in office, two governors and two representatives are known by many colored people to be stained. THE FABRIC OF AMERICA MUST INDEED BE SOILED.

"The secrets of American finance and government are known by ex-colored. The bourbon South receives ex-colored men within their undefiled and unsullied homes. The hospitality of the South's table is shared by the ex-colored and the black Jekyll and Hyde.

"They come back to us and smile and wink knowingly.

"THE SINS OF AMERICAN SIRES ARE BEING VISITED ON THE THIRD AND FOURTH GENERATION. THE MULATTO AND OCTOROON ARE PLANTING SEEDS IN AMERICA'S MOST FERTILE SOIL. IF BLACK BLOOD CAUSES DEGENERACY, AMERICA IS ENDANGERED AND IS POWERLESS TO PREVENT IT.

"How can you tell who is a Negro?"—*The Chicago Whip,* September 13.

VII. THE SOUTH AND THE NEGRO

THE following editorials and news items concern the general treatment of the Negro in his Southern home and the consequences of that treatment. In the foregoing sections nearly every topic brought this matter before the reader in some aspect or other: in these excerpts it comes before us mainly in its economic aspect. Sectional interests and not wholly racial interests may have determined the character of some of the utterances. In general, however, we may assume race loyalty in the writers.

The first two editorials quoted appeared at the same date, the first in a Northern, the second in a Southern paper. They are representative. The reader may scrutinize them for a difference.

"The Southern Credo

There has been heard a great deal of talk recently from timid, scared or venal colored men about the Southern white people being the best friends the Negro has in this country. We have pointed out who these men are and just why they talk as they do. It is to be noted that none of this sort of talk has been engaged in by colored women. We have yet to hear of a single colored woman being either frightened or bribed into forswearing the rights for which the race has been fighting all these years or into lauding the well defined policy of oppression and injustice of the South as something satisfactory to the Negro and for the best interests of the race.

"And this fact about the colored women simply confirms us in the opinion we have before expressed in these columns, that it is the women who always have been and still are the mainstay and the chief hope of the race. Taken as a whole, the colored women are braver than the men and less liable to being bought off. They are more loyal, more self-sacrificing and more earnest as workers in all things pertaining to the welfare of the the race. If there is any worthwhile movement among Negroes in this country which does not have to depend chiefly upon the women to keep it going, the writer would like to hear about it.

"Getting back to our subject, what is there to all this talk about the Southern white man being the Negro's best friend? Absolutely nothing but bunk. It is true that certain Southern white men are friendly to certain Negroes. A white man of this class will lend a certain Negro money, will give him a job and will afford him a protection somewhat of the kind the old feudal lords used to afford their serfs. But this same white man while he is doing all this for a certain Negro because he looks on him as one of 'my Negroes' will have not the remotest idea of according fairness and justice and opportunity to Negroes as a race, as men and women, as citizens of a common country.

"Perhaps there isn't a white man in the South who is not friendly toward at least one Negro. Even the men who lead mobs and lynchings and burnings at the stake, and even those —and they are the worst of all—who pass and maintain laws to rob and oppress the Negro race, they all have their certain Negroes toward whom they are friendly, whom they will help, to whom they will lend money and give a job.

"It is this seeming paradox in Southern character which misleads some colored people into thinking that, after all, the white man of the South is the Negro's best friend. We have heard colored men try to balance all the harm that Ben Tillman did to the race by pointing to the fact that he kept a colored foreman on his plantation in South Carolina. This is looking at the question through a pin hole. Ben Tillman used up the greater part of all the physical and mental strength he had in trying to keep the Negro race down. He used all the talent he possessed in ridiculing and vilifying and degrading the Negro race in the United States Senate and on platforms throughout the country. If Ben Tillman had been the benefactor of a hundred or a thousand colored foremen on as many plantations, it would not have been a counterbalance to his attitude on the Negro as a race.

"Regardless of all the cases of individual kindness and friendliness shown by Southern white people to certain colored people, it is clear to anybody with common sense that it is the firm intention of Southern white people as a class never to allow Negroes as a race to either enjoy the rights or become citizens or men in the fullest sense of the terms.

"An editorial in a recent issue of 'The Shreveport (La.) Times' states the Southern credo on the Negro question as clearly as we have ever seen it put by one of that class of Southern white men claiming to be the Negro's best friend. The whole article is written in a vein of friendly advice to the Negro, and by a writer professing to have the best interests of the race at heart. We should like to quote the whole editorial in order to show how a Southern white man who is utterly opposed to any development on the part of the race toward full citizenship and manhood can fool himself into believing that he is the Negro's best friend. But the whole article is too long. We, therefore, quote only the following paragraph:

" 'We venture to say that fully ninety per cent of all the race troubles in the South are the result of the Negro forgetting his place. If the black man will stay where he belongs, act like a Negro should act, work like a Negro should work, talk like a Negro should talk, and study like a Negro should study, there will be very few riots, fights or clashes. Instead of the "societies" and "unions" floating propaganda to "lead" the Negro to "independency" or to lift them up to the plane of the white man, they should foster education that will instill in the Negro the desire, and impress upon him the NECESSITY of keeping his place.'

"There it is clear and plain. Those are the terms on which the white man in the South will be friendly to the Negro. There may be cases in which colored men feel that they are obliged to accept favors on these terms; however, they need not feel obliged to proclaim to the world that they are satisfied, and that the men who grant them the favors are their best friends.

"The Negro in the United States has got to face this fact: his best and highest future he has got to work out against and not with the present attitude of the Southern white man. We are not saying that there are not some individual Southern white men who have the best and highest future of the Negro in view, but they are so few as to be negligible."—*The New York Age*, November 1.

"The Temper of Rural Life

"The fortune of the rural white in the southland has always been inseparably dependent and interwoven with that of the rural Negro. There is no prosperous community of the south that is not predicated to a very large extent upon its black labor, while the principal southern industries, including agriculture, lumbering, mining and naval stores are helplessly impossible without it. Any one will admit that seventy percent of the labor of the rural south has been done by the Negro hands, even if directed by white heads.

"It is worse than folly then that there should exist here anything but the most abiding interest in the welfare of this essential increment of labor—to see that it is satisfied, protected, secured in the possession of its earnings and encouraged in every way. It seems foolish that anything should be allowed to intervene to terrorize, affright and scatter this labor.

"And yet, we have the curious and inconsistent spectacle of the rural white south making the agricultural communities uninhabitable and unbearable for the Negro, and driving him to the cities and to the north. Investigations of thousands of Negroes who have left the farming districts have disclosed many reasons for their leaving, but the most universal reason given has been the terror of physical violence, this even outweighing the insecurity of property and the failure of justice in the courts. These conclusions are based on a sociological survey made for the government by four white men and a Negro, the whites being principally southern men.

"It is already becoming difficult and will soon be next to impossible for white men in rural communities to hire Negroes as wage-hands or engage them as tenants. We dare predict that another generation will remove the Negro as a wage hand and tenant or share-cropper, unless rural conditions take a radical change for the better. It is also true that, in spite of the intimidation to which they are subjected, the Negro owning his farm, the accumulation of a life time in many cases, will continue for a longer time.

"Now, even if the motives of humanitarianism and simple justice do not dictate a different policy with regard to the labor in rural districts, it would seem that purely selfish, economic reasons would militate to cause a change in these rough tactics employed by the semi-civilized terrorists in rural communities. If, indeed, there be any good people left in the farming areas, or if being there they are courageous to assert the right and sensible and business-like handling of their Negro labor, it seems time that they should come to the fore.

"The young Negro is leaving for the cities or for the north.

where better conditions, embracing good schools, better wages, safety of person and property and wider social opportunity, await him. It is well established that the right and privilege to spend a dollar at highest purchasing power must go along with the chance to earn it.

"The Negro preacher and teacher and merchant are leaving because their business is gone. These leaders of the group have preached the doctrine of law and order and thrift as means of insuring justice and protection, only to see their doctrines proved to be idlest folly by severest oppression and persecution on every hand. They too have only acted normally wherever they have moved to healthier conditions.

"There is no white man of the south, who has investigated it, who does not know that the charges alleged against Negroes by the rough-necks of rural·communities where mobs are made, are mostly false and always highly colored. A Savannah policeman, his imaginative faculty doing over-time, conjured up in his brain a terrible situation at the Union Station a few days ago. He sent in a riot call, which caused much excitement. Upon investigation, no one saw any semblance of riot save himself. Such vivid imaginations breed trouble. In the rural districts the slightest occurrence is fanned into a consuming flame of hate, destruction and death. by such men. And there are thousands of them all over the land, and they have the thinkers and those who would do justice backed off. They put words into the mouths of the law-abiding and keep them silent and unthinking.

"What are we coming to?

"Lynching is increasing by numbers and in brutality. Lynching is the penalty for any charge. All the Negroes are terrorized or driven from their homes in a given community for the infraction of an individual. Prosperous self-respecting Negroes conceded to be good citizens by all are ordered to sell their possessions and get out.

"And the law-abiding white citizens, few and unassertive, do not dare to raise their hands and they speak safely and fearfully, if at all.

"This is just where the alarm comes in. It would seem that the fair and just and human personnel of the white south is 'on the run' or subdued. Many of these, hitherto at least fair, have been whipped into the ranks of those who abuse, take advantage and oppress.

"Many Negroes, now including those who have accumulated

competencies and modest fortunes and reared fine families, are leaving to settle in northern centers, where there is at least a fighting chance to survive the mob, and where innocent men, women and children are not slaughtered.

"Negroes are driven to the point of desperation or to flight and many are wisely taking the latter."—*The Savannah Tribune*, November 1.

The Louisville News, October 18, presents a serious aspect of the emigration of the Negro from the South. Numerous reports and comments are to the same effect:

"The Man Higher Up

Talks with progressive members of the Race who are passing this way leaving the South bring out the startling revelations that there is a propaganda in the South against the intelligent property-owning, well-to-do black man.

"It has been thought heretofore that lynching, horsewhipping, chain-ganging and such methods of 'Southern justice' were practiced only on the shiftless, worthless, ignorant and vicious 'Negro.' But it develops that this is the kind of Colored men wanted.

"Arkansas, Alabama and Mississippi daily furnish examples of fraud and persecution of the black man who has something, who knows something and who stands for something. A common ruse is to charge a man of means and property with improper relations with a white woman. He is then hounded out of town and his property sold at a sacrifice or completely confiscated. Appeals to leading whites are of no avail, for they are aiding and abetting the whole thing. What the answer is we cannot say. Surely the worm will turn. It means that not only will Colored labor leave the South, but Colored capital as well, and, strange as it may seem, Colored capital is no inconsiderable thing in the South."

The efforts of the South, through appeals and write-ups in the Associated Press and through commissions sent North and commissions brought South, to induce the Negroes to return home have generally been met with ridicule and irony in the colored press. One example must suffice. The following article was widely printed:

"SOUTH AFTER NEGROES

Propaganda Through Associated Press to Induce Return—No Change in Conditions

The Mississippi Welfare League is making desperate efforts to develop a replacement scheme for bringing back Negroes from the North. Daily the Associated Press is made use of to circulate throughout the country their propaganda, which consists of the advertisement of the Mississippi Welfare League and the report of a certain commission of Chicago Negroes carried to the state in the hope of inducing Negroes to come back. A shortage of labor has been experienced for over two years. It is stated that provisions are being made to provide a means of return to thousands of Negroes before the winter sets in. Leading cities in the Delta, including Greenwood, Clarkdale, Greenville, Indianola, Leland and others are giving full support and assurances of coöperation with a scheme to accomplish their return.

THE MISSION REPORTS

"During August Jack C. Wilson, executive leader of the Mississippi Welfare League, visited Chicago to go into the labor question, to study possibilities for returning Negroes, to communicate with every source of information and to formulate recommendations. Mr. Wilson spent ten days in Chicago. He reported that 'men in politics' declined to give help and every obstacle was placed in his way. Mr. Wilson returned disappointed, but carried with him a commission composed of Negroes to study conditions in the South.

REPORT OF THE COLORED MISSION

"Three Chicago Negroes were piloted through the South by Mr. Wilson and permitted to talk with selected Negroes. They were permitted to see only what had been prepared for them by being carried around in automobiles. They reported that 'railroad accommodations for Negroes were adequate and uniform irrespective of locality'; that treatment accorded Negro passengers by railroad officials was courteous throughout; that Negroes were prosperous, some owning as much as $175,000 worth of property and average $1,500 a year on their crops;

that public school terms were nine months in the city and eight months in the country for white and colored alike; that many modern homes are being built for Negroes, and that the strongest possible human ties between planter and worker exist. They reported that in no instance were the Negroes not given the freest use of sidewalks, streets and thoroughfares and that they were unable to find any trace of friction of any kind between the races.

NORTH MISREPRESENTED

"Comparing these false reports with Chicago, it is stated that on one day 17,000 Negroes were in the bread line in August and that conditions are to be worse this winter.

URBAN LEAGUE ACTS

"The Chicago Urban League, an organization which has devoted its effort largely to the adjusting of migrants from the South, was solicited by representatives from Mississippi and Louisiana. Its policies in regard to the industrial placements are careful and strict. No Negroes are sent or advised to go into any industry or locality to live where it has not first been determined that conditions warrant it. It immediately set about to ascertain the truth of reports concerning the South. Reports from Mississippi on the activities of the commission and the situation in general are about as follows:

" 'The investigating committee of the alleged Negro leaders from Chicago was so very nauseating to us that I regret to refer to it. These fellows, whoever they were, were guarded by those who had charge of them as if they had been convicts. They were not even allowed to have the privilege of purchasing their own tickets. The chief thing they found here was that we were "allowed to walk on the sidewalks."

" 'Let me assure you once and for all that racial conditions are worse in the South to-day than they have been in all the years of my life, all of which have been spent here, and any one who reports to the contrary is false and a traitor to the cause of humanity.

" 'Since our boys returned from the front it appears that every white man has a chip on his shoulder. Lynchings occur for less trivial offenses, burnings are more frequent, privileges are curtailed and feeling is very, very bitter.

" 'My advice to any race man who can make bread across

the line is that he remain there, and it would be an outrage for the people to be deceived and brought back here.'

"From Louisiana, the state represented in Chicago by a committee from the New Orleans Chamber of Commerce and Mr. Denechaud, director of the department of Immigration for the state, the following report is returned:

" 'The commissions have an entirely different way of viewing the state of affairs here from the way Negroes on the ground here view it. I have interviewed Negro laborers, Negro mechanics, Negro porters, Negro chauffeurs, Negro house servants, male and female; Negro ministers of the gospel, Negro pharmacists, Negro physicians and surgeons, Negro landlords, business men, planters and farmers and Negro pharmacists, Negro physicians come back from service in the United States army and navy and been back long enough to be competent to answer from observation and experience, also men in the various branches of the federal civil service, and I have been unable to discover one who would agree that he finds conditions better now than they were a year or so ago for the Negroes, or even one who said that he had heard that some other Negro here said conditions were improved at all. The answers I got on the question: "Are conditions now any better than they were before the war for the Negroes?" have run like this, to wit:

" ' "Some deceitful, lying Negroes may say times are better, but he would at the same time know that he was not telling the truth."

" ' "Ain't all the judges, all the police and constables, all the juries white men as ever? Does the word of a Negro count for more now than it did before the war Don't white men insult our wives and daughters and our sisters and get off at it unless when we take the law into our own hand and punish them for it ourselves and get lynched for protecting our own just as often as ever?"

" 'It is ridiculous, not to say absurd, for any Negro to say he finds conditions better here. Don't you remember that Negroes answering an invitation to meet a welfare committee of white men not long ago were told as soon as they got into the meeting place that the committee was ready to hear what Negroes wanted, but that the question of the Negro's right to exercise the right of voting would not be allowed to be discussed at all and that that must be agreed to before any discussion whatever would be entertained, and that the Negroes left the meeting place without a chance to demand the one main thing that they wished to enjoy?'

"Negroes may use their own judgment and discretion in comparing these reports."

Several of the many phases of the subject will be found presented in the following articles:

"Cracker Reasoning and Cracker Law

"'CESSATION OF LYNCHING'
"'EQUAL SCHOOL FACILITIES'
"'EQUALITY AT THE POLLS'
"'EQUAL ACCOMMODATIONS ON RAILROADS'

"For advocating this program of the National Association for the Advancement of Colored People before the courts of Austin, Texas, John R. Shillady, white, National Secretary of the Association, was waylaid on his way from the meeting to his hotel and severely beaten. The men who assaulted him were Dave J. Pickle, county judge, Charles Hamby, constable, and Ben Pierce, all of them white, together with several thugs.

" 'Judge' Pickle issued a statement after the fight to the effect that Mr. Shillady was guilty of advocating 'social equality' for the colored people of Austin, and that he 'whipped him and ordered him to leave the city, for the best interest of the state.'

"Governor Hobby of Texas who was appealed to in the interest of law and order by the Association sent the reply: 'Shillady was the only offender, and was punished before your telegram came.'

"This is the case, and on its face, it seems that the county judge, sworn to uphold the law, thinks he has the right as a private citizen to beat up another citizen on the public street, ORDER him to leave the city, and this in the interest of the state. Likewise Governor Hobby believes that 'Judge' Pickle was entirely within the law in administering an assault, and the law is entirely satisfied in making no effort to punish the judge,—BECAUSE CRIME WAS COMMITTED BY SHILLADY IN COMING TO TEXAS, AND REPRESENTATIVES OF THE N. A. A. C. P. SHOULD STAY OUT OF THE STATE.

"This is Cracker Reasoning and more than this it is Cracker Law.

"It is best expressed in the words of Representative Byrnes of South Carolina in the House this week, who, speaking on mob law, said:

" 'THE WHITE MAN DOES NOT REASON, HE ACTS.

" 'FOR ANY NEGRO, WHO HAS BECOME INNOCULATED WITH THE DESIRE FOR POLITICAL EQUALITY, THERE IS NO EMPLOYMENT FOR HIM IN THE SOUTH, NOR IS THERE ANY ROOM FOR HIM IN THE SOUTH.

" 'THIS IS A WHITE MAN'S COUNTRY AND WILL ALWAYS REMAIN A WHITE MAN'S COUNTRY.'

"When a so-called Representative rises to utter such bunk in the Congress of the United States, it is enough to make the blood of every righteous man boil with indignation. America cannot be safe for the Negro, nor can it long be safe for the white man, until it relegates to oblivion—the resting place of Vardaman and Tillman—violators of law and order.

"It is to be hoped that the National Association and Secretary Shillady will not allow any intimidation to interfere with their organization of strong branches of the Association in every Southern town. The fight is on. The goal is citizenship rights for every Negro in the United States. A cracker Senator beat Charles Sumner on the floor of the Senate because the latter urged political equality of the Negro, but that did not stop the addition of the 14th and the 15th Amendments to the constitution.

"And no more can Pickles and Byrnes, by violence and threats of violence, stop to-day the irresistible flood of public opinion that is solid for the rights of the Negro under the constitution."—*The Afro-American* (Baltimore), August 29.

"WANT TO DRIVE BACK SOUTH

Southern Afro-Americans in the North

The insidious policy of holding up the black man as a brute was begun in France immediately after the glorious record made by the colored soldiers. The policy that dominated the American army was Southern and the treatment accorded colored people in the south was the treatment prejudiced southern white army officers attempted to put in force in France. The French did not accept the southern policy. The southern white soldier became the disseminator of this virus of 'Negro bestiality.' Coming to America these same southern soldiers sought with renewed assurance of success to cover America with 'hatred toward colored people.' To do this the south was craven enough to drag into the mire the character of the white woman. The southern press became the mouthpiece of this horde of race detractors. White male brutes blackened their faces and mated with white women with the express understanding that they, the white women, would join with them in crying 'rape by black men.' Reports of dozens of cases, without apprehension or conviction, were circulated in order that public sentiment might be 'educated' to accept any atrocity white men might place upon colored men. This was over-worked in Washington as well as in Omaha. The men at the bottom of these riots were southern white men of the basest sort—'crackers.' The iniquity of their scheme is apparent when after these outbreaks in the north, southern papers join in inviting Negroes to return south as the south is willing to accept them. Then, too, if the south can say to colored people leaving and going north, that northern people are worse toward you than southern people, this would have a tendency to discourage Negroes from leaving the south. Economic reasons are behind this vicious propaganda. Southern white men are sent north for the very purpose of destroying the law of the north as they have destroyed it in the south. Southern men in the U. S. Congress are parties to this system of peonage, race oppression and law-breaking. A U. S. Senator 'justified' the Omaha tragedy. He 'justified' it as a 'means of protecting white women.' We venture the assertion that ninety-five per cent of the outrages reported in Omaha were committed, if at all, by white men. Besides, readers of the press see daily occurrences of white men outraging even thirteen-year-old white and black girls. Southern Senators should shut their mouths and cover over their nakedness in this matter. We oppose the seduction and forcing of any woman by any man, but the sins committed by white men of the south against colored women have never been expiated for. The very complexion of the colored people largely shows the bestiality of the southern white 'man.' Back of all this cry of rape is the fixed purpose of withdrawing the attention of the north from the iniquity of the south in ballot-box thievery, peonage, brutality, murder and unjust representation in the National Congress and Electoral College so that they may

again be able to steal the presidency. We assert that there
is not a Senator from the south that holds his seat through an
honest election. Every southern state by intimidation, force,
brutality and ballot-box stuffing, thwarts the will of the people.
Colored men are not allowed to vote. There can be no honest
election until colored men like all other citizens be allowed to
vote as they choose, and their votes counted as cast. The south
might as well know now as later that colored men will fight
them until their strangle-hold on the American government is
relaxed. The world does not believe their lies. Their injustice toward the Negroes and the northern whites, under the
present Administration, convicts them of being unworthy to be
trusted. The south must be put out of business or America is
a destroyed nation."   (Rev.) Wm. A. Byrd.
              —*The Cleveland Gazette,* October 11.

"The Real Cause of Unrest Among Negroes in the South

Any man who has been in the South knows that the housing
conditions of our people are poor both in the country and towns.
Many a country tenant home is without a glass window light,
with wooden window shutters on hinges, with holes in the
floors and walls large enough for cats and dogs to pass in
and out, and with from 6 to 12 and 15 in a 2, 3, or 4 room
house, but this is not the most grievous. With the salary of
our teachers so low until a professional teacher will have to
leave his profession or decide to sacrifice nearly all the neces-
sities of life that he might help his or her people; the plantation
owner is the trustee of the Negro School or in other words he
is the 'sole boss' of the situation and the school only runs
when there is nothing going on on the farm—that is, every
child that is large enough to do anything at all must come out
of school and take his or her place in the field, but this is not
the most grievous thing that causes the unrest. Although the
Negro is exposed to every wrath and indignation of the white
man with no police protection, he thinks, by his doing more than
is necessary, he can escape; but exposure to the whims of that
element of whites who do not think is not his biggest grievance. His biggest grievance, his real grievance is the systematic robbery of him out of his labor. In the first place, the
courts are against him, so he has no redress and no lawyer

will dare to handle his case. The Chamber of Commerce and Elk's Hall are places to meet and regulate this system of robbery. Some plantations that furnish money, usually charge unreasonable interest; charge from $8.00 to $18.00 per acre for the land, then sell the Negro's cotton or allow so much for it; and if the commissary furnishes he is charged 2 and 3 times as much for the commonest of food and then interest on that,—that is, they will allow the Negro tenant 5, 10 or 15c less than market price and take the seeds for a Christmas gift. Some plantations, the Negro is only told what is coming to him or how much more he owes without a statement of how much of this he has used and it is sudden death if he attempts to ascertain the reason for his success or failure. He and his family made the cotton and he and his family picked it out and put it in the cotton house and that moment he and his family's interest ceased and the white man's started. Then the Negro can't question this procedure. Now, there is nearly a permanent agreement that all plantations must either act alike or not interfere with the labor on the other's plantation, so the Negro is forced to stay there to watch himself and his family systematically robbed every year; first, from a good house; second, from a good school; third, from human protection by the officers; and, fourth, from the very life of his man power, which is more than he can bear. This is the cause of the biggest unrest. When a man makes his bread be he black or white and just before time for him to eat, he is robbed without a redress, is more than he can stand. He feels, if I could just get the worth of my labor I could make out, but my poor family is robbed of everything. This is why he is seeking a change, and he is not moving like he is going to move unless this system is changed. A human chance is the only royal road the Negro wishes to travel, you must let him have it or count the days he has been gone."—*The Negro Star* (Wichita), October 24.

"The Press despatches this week say that the Southern newspaper Publishers' Association would spend a hundred thousand dollars this year advertising the South. 'Tisn't necessary, brother, your rough necks and lynchers have advertised the South so thoroughly that there isn't any danger or possibility of any immigration setting in toward that benighted section of our fair land. Clean up, put down lynching, break your young white 'bloods' away from their Negro mistresses, cut out your vicious Jim Crow and give every man a square deal and then you'll not be wasting money advertising your 'beloved South.'—*The Kansas City* [Mo.] *Sun,* October 25.

Doubtless the writer of the following editorial is a Negro whose "heart turns back to Dixie," but whose footsteps lead not that way:

"There is no question that the Negro naturally prefers the south. That he has remained there in such numbers in spite of the ill treatment he has received, is proof positive of that. Ask almost any one of the recent migrants the reason for his leaving the south and he will tell you that, which, in its final analysis, is a denial of opportunities accorded all other peoples. 'Tis one thing to 'know' the Negro and quite another thing to 'be' a Negro and feel the sting in being such.

"That the Colored people of the south are 'actually making progress, accumulating money, buying property and educating their children' is to their credit, not to that of their locus. It is in spite of the handicaps, not because of them. But what good is money and property when its value is less than that of other people who have less; when it is unable to protect one from insult or secure the consideration of the poorest white citizen? Down in Houston, Tex., Mrs. Libbie Bautte, a teacher in the Colored schools, had a safety deposit box in the Union National Bank of that city. The usual notice that the rent of $3.00 would be due on May 14th was addressed to 'Libbie Bautte Nig' and the envelope containing the notice addressed the same.

"The Sentinel man does not need to accept Mr. Byrnes' analysis. He needs but to turn to the columns of his own paper to find the cause of the discontent. No black man is absolutely safe in the south. He knows that if not to-day, it may be to-morrow he will be called upon to pay the supreme sacrifice for daring to dispute the word of a white man. We know whereof we speak because we have lived there. In the breast of the average southerner is a deep-seated resentment against all Colored people because of the Emancipation Proclamation. Even if there were no so-called 'leaders,' the treatment accorded the Colored people is enough to breed discontent among angels. It is being noticed now because they have the manhood to resent it—a healthy change."—*The Wisconsin Weekly Blade* (Madison), September 18.

"The Afro-American Side of the Case

. . . .

The dissatisfaction and unrest that is so often and so unfortunately manifesting itself, and that is beginning of late to express itself in armed resistance to violence, had its first real expression in the wholesale migration of Afro-Americans from the South during 1916 and 1917. Southern papers then said it was the lure of high wages and promises of 'social equality' that caused them to move out of the South in such large numbers, but as usual the press was mistaken. The Negroes arose without leaders and with no other objective in view except freedom and marched away from lynching and mob violence, starvation wages, peonage, poor schools, injustice in the courts and other oppressive conditions, because they could no longer endure these conditions and no longer feel that their lives were safe in the Southland. True, their presence in the North in large numbers is causing race riots in many instances, and in some instances they are meeting conditions not much better than those they fled to escape, but their flight is going to ultimately awaken the conscience of this nation to the wrongs they suffer or bathe a good portion of it in blood.

"When Afro-Americans in the South protest against mob violence and lynching the Southern press and Southern statesmen befuddle the issue by proclaiming that if Negroes would stop the one unmentionable crime, lynching would stop, and they excuse lynching and dismiss the subject. As a matter of fact only one-fifth of the lynchings that occur in the whole country are caused by assaults upon women. Just a few days ago five Afro-Americans were lynched in Georgia because one had committed murder, and a few weeks ago an old colored man, seventy years of age, was lynched because he defended two colored women against the attacks of two white drunken men in his own home. These occurrences are minimized, while the occasional assault is elaborated on and magnified. Afro-Americans do not sympathize with the brute who violates a woman, white or black, or who commits any other form of lawlessness, but every Afro-American knows that no Afro-American is safe as long as the rule of the mob is. allowed to take the place of the constituted legal authorities.

"The cause of Afro-American unrest is plain to any one who wants to face the truth, and has the courage to face it and admit it."—*The Journal and Guide* (Norfolk, Va.), October 11.

A contributed article in *The Christian Index* (Jackson, Tenn.), September 11, deals at length with peonage in the South. I take the middle third of the article:

"In almost every county in Georgia and nearly every community in these counties there is a cunning device that can easily be termed as peonage; carried on by some leading white farmers, and public workers and what is true in Georgia is true of the common Southland. It is on the following order:

"In small towns and in cities of lesser size where city courts and superior courts are held from time to time, these farmers and 'public work' firms have, it seems, an understanding with the court officials, whereby they (when colored men and boys and women are convicted of petty crimes) pay their fines, take these unfortunate folks into custody and keep them indefinitely. This kind of practice has built up a perfect system of peonage in Georgia and the South. In a certain county in Georgia white men go into crowds of colored young men and encourage and pursuade them to commit crime with the promise of 'paying them out.' I know of instances where white men have persuaded colored men to kill one another, just to see if these certain white men could not influence the court and buy or get the prisoner out, to take to the farm to work it out.

"In another county I know of a colored man who has been working on a certain plantation for 10 years with a large family, running a 4 horse farm and coming out in debt every year, while still another man bargained to work his large family of 5 boys and 7 girls 'for the 5th' of the crop and after picking 30 bales of cotton and 500 bushels of corn, etc., was told the crops were short and that there would be 'no 5th' that year and that the poor fellow owed the white man $50.00 and he must have his money! I know of another case where a white man raped a poor colored man's daughter, the girl went home, told her father, the poor father went and asked the white man about it, and was cursed out and ordered home and to 'shut his mouth.' I advised this poor man to talk it over with the white men who stood for something in his community. He was told that they could do him no good; I sent then to the white minister of the community and the white minister said to him 'if he went to law he would be laughed out of court and would be otherwise run out of the community, etc.'

"In another case a white man went to a colored father and

ordered him to send his daughter up to the big house to become the 'common wife' of this white man, so the father sent his daughter off to another city which, when the white man found it out, he ordered the girl to be brought back and sent up to him as he first commanded and it was done because this colored man had a large plantation near this white man and he did not want to break up and move away. These are a few instances of the peonage system of the South."

"Colored Man Arrested for Inducing People to Leave 'South'

New Orleans, Aug. 21.—There is a state law in Louisiana which prevents labor agents from securing laborers in that state and shipping them to points out of its boundaries.

"The first arrest for the violation of this order was that of Mondane Jones, colored, who was taken into custody and charged with violation of the above law.

"Jones, it is alleged, was shipping people of his color to points outside of the state from the town of Bessemer. When arrested he was making arrangements at the depot of the Alabama Great Southern Railroad. A large number of men and women were at the station preparing to leave when the labor agent was taken in charge.

"There were many labor agents in Bessemer who were doing a big business until this so-called law, violating the constitutional rights of the people, went into effect. The labor agents have all left town, fearing that they would receive the same treatment handed Jones."—*The Whip* (Chicago), August 21.

The following editorial from *The Charleston* [S. C.] *Messenger,* September 6, strikes a different note from the rest, it will be perceived. Here, it seems, the soul of the Southern black man speaks to the soul of the Southern white man—more in bitterness of sorrow than in bitterness of hate.

"The Call of the South

A few years ago labor agents were in the south persuading Negro laborers to go north to supply the needs of that labor market. To-day it is said that southern labor agents are in the north ready to pay transportation for all Negro laborers who are willing to return south. This change of conditions and appeal to Negro labor from both sides of the old Mason and Dixon line shows that the Negro is still in demand as a laborer. He is still wanted. No one else has been found to take his place or bear the burdens that he has carried upon his shoulders for generations. The migration of Negro laborers to the north in the last five years caused the transfer of five hundred thousand members of the race from one section of the country to the other. The nation now watches to see if this result is to be permanent or only temporary. Certain birds go from Florida to Canada every spring, but the call of the south brings them back in the fall. There are those who look upon the Negro as a natural and permanent resident of the south and believe that no matter where he may travel, some day he will be coming back to Dixie. There are many reasons why the call of the south makes a strong appeal to the average Negro. It is a call to come back home. His earliest memories are of the south, he sings southern songs, he dreams of the scenery of the southland. He is familiar with its life and its customs. It is a land where he has relatives and friends and graves that are dear. There are very few Negroes who have grown to manhood in the south that do not boast of at least one good white friend in his home town or community. The old home spirit makes a strong appeal to human nature and the colored man is no exception to the general rule.

"Not only labor agents but also governors of different states, business organizations and many of the leading newspapers of the South are now joining in this cordial invitation to Negroes who have left the South to return back home from the far country into which they have wandered and where some of them have recently had 'riotous' living thrust upon them. This call of the South reminds the colored man that in this portion of the country his people dwell in large numbers.

"In two states, many cities and a large number of counties they are in the majority. Here are the great Negro churches, schools, lodges and other organizations that mean much in the progress of the race. Here the colored people living in great numbers give a future hope of patronage for business enterprises and undertakings that will in time tend to make the race wealthy and independent. In the north there is no prospect of the colored element becoming more than a minor part of the population and business competition is so strong and conditions so unfavorable that the chances for success in any commercial line are very poor compared with the basis of patronage that the Negro business man has in the South.

"This new appeal to the Negro who has gone North from the South, also emphasizes a land of beauty, mild climate and comparatively cheap living. The short winters, the balmy air, the easily secured products from the field, the rivers and the forests are all temptations that naturally lead the colored migrant to put his foot in the path that will lead towards the old home and the plantation.

"Never before has such an appeal been made to the Negro by the leading men and the leading influence of the South. The very fact that they urge the Negro to return is significant. The South is consistent in this matter. It is opposed to his leaving. It favors his coming back. There are no lavish promises of conditions or compensation, but every one must realize that wages are better in the South now than at any time for both black and white. The Negro who returns will find wages better than when he left. More money is being put into Negro schools in the South than ever before, and even the millionaires of the North who give thousands of dollars for Negro education seem inclined to spend it at Hampton, Tuskegee and other schools for the race in the South.

"The Negro who returns will find his people making progress in the South. He will find more Negro banks, insurance companies, real estate firms and other enterprises than at any other time in the history of the race.

"Such is the call of the South to the Negro who has gone North. Will he come back? If not, why not?"

The August number of *The Challenge Magazine* (Chicago), which under its title bears this legend: IT FEARS ONLY GOD: contained the following as its leading editorial:

"American Huns

The very worst German Hun cannot be so vile, inhuman, contaminative of every civilized instinct as the Huns of America who delight in standing with their families, children included, over the burning, stinking flesh of Negro men tied to trees or in public squares; or as those midnight devils that tear from the bellies of Black mothers their unborn babies and crush their soggy brains beneath their feet.

"The South is more Hellish than Germany ever was even under the 'tyrannical régime' of the Kaiser. The South in the Twentieth Century stoops to atrocities that only the South can stoop to without shame or remorse; from which Germany would recoil in loathing and disgust. In four years of war, the most barbarous known to history, taking every crime committed by German soldiers on peasant women, black robed priests, and Red Cross nurses, I can find none so black as the burning of young Loyd Clay at Vicksburg, Mississippi, in the LAND OF THE FREE AND THE HOME OF THE BRAVE.

"Assuming that there is or was a German Hun, he was the direct product of a consuming conflict of human forces in which little was ever done fairly by either side, in which all men, in the armies, submitting to degenerate impulses spouting under and propagated by abnormal passions sank their very souls in the murky blood pits of human shame and human disaster, destroying without compunction the frail bodies of women along with the bodies of men. Yet there is no record of a German doing a thing like the following: 'When the body was hoisted up from the ground coal oil was poured on the Negro's head and a match applied. The Negro's hands were loose when he was strung up, and he began to climb up the rope, but he was lowered and his hands tied. As the mob moved from the jail to the scene of the lynching a number of women joined the procession and witnessed the proceedings. Tormented by the flames that lapped his legs and reached his trunk, strangled by the noose, his limbs jerked from below, Loyd Clay, young Negro of twenty-four years, made no outcry. He lifted his arms, placed his palms together in an attitude of prayer, but made no sound. As the flames burned higher and higher, he raised his legs, doubling them under him in a vain effort to escape the blaze.' This is the doing of American Huns.

"The 'German Hun' is beaten but the world is made no safer for Democracy. Humanity has been defended, but lifted no higher. Democracy never will be safe in America until these occurrences are made impossible either by the proper execution of the law or with double barrel shot guns. Humanity never will be lifted any higher in America until Negro men and women, as well as white, are made 'secure in their

life and property.' I hate every Hun, and the worst I know
are the ones that thrive under the free institutions of America."

Much has appeared in the Colored papers about the opportunities now offered the race in other countries. The following editorial on this topic is from *The Favorite Magazine*
(Chicago), November:

"The Auction Block

The Negro will always be in the mire so long as he is
forced to dwell beside his enemy, the poor white of the South.
In the first place, the poor white is crude and ignorant and
lacks the ability to appreciate what the Negro is doing and has
done for the South. All the trouble the Negro has undergone
has been due to this detestable creature who has not contributed
one iota to civilization.

"The South is far from being the best place for the Negro.
Any community that oppresses its citizens is unworthy of those
citizens' loyalty. Any community that burns men and women
at the stake is too far beneath the level of civilization to claim
the allegiance of the most Christian-like races on earth.

"There are many ports of refuge for us. Not only the North,
but foreign countries are calling us. France, glorious France,
in whose sunny clime Dumas was nurtured, offers us both economic and social opportunities. Latin America, the garden of
the world, offers us all the golden privileges of a land that
has never known race prejudice. Mexico is willing not only
to give us the privileges of Mexican citizenship, but will cham-
pion our cause.

"How foolish it is for us to cling to a community that cracks
the slave whip over us when we have such golden opportunities
awaiting us in other lands! How foolish it is for us to be
singing 'Dixie' when we can be singing the 'Marseillaise'
or 'Marching Through Georgia!' How foolish it is for us
to be forever cringing to the Southern white man when we can
be welcomed in communities that value the black man the
same as the white man. Let us be friends with those who are
our friends and repudiate those who are our enemies.

"If you want us, beloved France, we are ready to take up our
beds, make our home with you and fight your battles, as our
African cousins and our own boys did in the Great War. If

you want us, Mexico, we are ready to become your citizens and willing to do all we can to make you a great power among the nations. If you want us, Latin America, we are ready to dwell among you and make you rich as we have made the Southern white man rich. If you want us, Mother Africa, we are ready to return home and eat the fatted calf; but unlike other prodigal sons, we are willing to raise more calves to enrich you in the eyes of the world.

"In other words, the Negro is on the auction block, and the nation or community that bids the highest will receive him."

VIII. THE NEGRO AND LABOR UNIONISM AND BOLSHEVISM

THE economic aspect of the race question is coming to be uppermost. In one colored paper I saw it estimated that the loss to the South in man-labor by the exodus of Negroes northward was equal in value to an entire Southern state. That the Negro fully appreciates his own economic value, and his strategic position, there is plenty of evidence in his papers.

The indisposition of the Negro to join labor unions, to participate in strikes, or in any way to foment trouble is frequently commented upon in his papers. On the other hand he has frequently been accused lately of being open to Bolshevistic propaganda and some of his magazines of the North have been arraigned. To these accusations the answer is here given in his own words.

On this subject there has been no end of editorial comment, because the Negro here as elsewhere is on the defensive. This is not to deny a friendliness to bolshevism and I. W. W.ism on the part of certain colored papers and magazines. I believe there are a few white papers with similar inclinations. The whole range of the colored press will be represented in the quotations that follow.

"If there is the least danger of the Negro race being influenced by revolutionary propaganda against the existing institutions of the country, what is the best preventive measure that could be taken? The answer is so easy that no one really needs to be told. Stop the lynchings and burnings of Negroes! Prove that the law was made for them as well as for other citizens, that the government will protect the black in the most elementary rights as well as the white."

149

This is the language of one paper, the sentiment of more than three hundred. Time and time again, throughout the colored press, I have met with this appeal, only expressed with more elaboration.

"When a Negro is a Bolshevist

Until recently no one would have thought of calling Negroes Bolshevists, and yet the Negro is no different now from what he has been with respect to his duty toward his government. He has always been a loyal citizen, and he is none the less loyal now. Just one thing has happened.

"Heretofore, any one, at any time, who cared to pick upon the Negro did so without fear of opposition from the Negro or criticism from the indifferent world. For years, the American white man has been heaping insult upon the Negro, and the Negro in turn has been returning his habitual smile for every insult.

"When the Negro was deprived of his ballot in the South, he just smiled and passed on. When he was made to slave all year for a share of the crops that never were divided, he just smiled and continued to labor and to pray. When the school system of the South was so manipulated that the white children received nine months' training and the Negro children received two and one-half months the Negro just smiled and prayed. The white man never thought of the Negro as a Bolshevist during all these trying times in the Negro's life. If the Negro was stabbed and bled, as long as he took the punishment without making any outcry, he was a good citizen and a loyal American. It has been a matter of common acceptance among white men that the Negro is peaceful, law abiding and in the main harmless and inoffensive. This reputation was won chiefly because the Negro offered no opposition to any insult or oppression. We never heard of a Negro Bolshevist as long as the Negro remained quiet.

"But when the Negro went to France and there laid down his life along with all other Americans for the salvation of France and the establishment of Democracy à la Wilson, they learned that any man who could, by his blood, purchase Liberty for France and Europe, could, by the shedding of enough of that same blood, purchase Liberty and Freedom for himself in his own country. When the Negro returned home and

Labor Unionism and Bolshevism   151

observed the attitude of the American white man toward him, when he observed the unhampered program of the lynchers operating without hindrance, he decided that the shedding of his blood in America in his own behalf differed very little from shedding his blood in France for Europe. He made his conclusions known by his acts. He at once began to fight back. He decided that Liberty is Liberty wherever found.

"Then went up the cry from all over the country: The Negro is joining the Bolshevists.

"The only conclusion, therefore, is: As long as the Negro submits to lynchings, burnings and oppressions—and says nothing, he is a loyal American citizen. But when he decides that lynchings and burnings shall cease even at the cost of some human bloodshed in America, then he is a Bolshevist."—*The Pittsburg Courier,* October 25.

"Bolshevist! ! !

Bolshevist is an epithet that present-day reactionaries delight to fling around loosely against those who insist on thinking for themselves and on agitating for their rights. We do not know exactly what the reactionaries desire to convey by the term—we do not think they know themselves. However, if as appears by its frequent use against those who are agitating in the people's interests and for justice for the oppressed, the term is intended to cover those "bad agitators," who are not content that the people shall forever be enslaved in the clutches of the cut-throat, child-exploiting, capitalist-imperialist crew, then assuredly we are Bolshevists. This epithet nor any other holds any terrors for us. If to fight for one's rights is to be Bolshevists, then we are Bolshevists and let them make the most of it!

"And for the further information of the asses who use the term so loosely we will make the statement that we would not for a moment hesitate to ally ourselves with any group, if by such an alliance we could compass the liberation of our race and the redemption of our Fatherland. A man pressed to earth by another with murderous intent is not under any obligation to choose his weapons. He would be a fool if he did not use any or whatever weapon was within his reach. Self-preservation is the first law of human nature."—*The Crusader* (New York), October.

That there is Bolshevistic propaganda among Negroes, and that there is a real danger, their editors admit, directly and indirectly. This admission, however, is made in order to warn the colored people against it and the white people against the conditions which favor it, conditions within their power to remedy.

The following editorial from *The Searchlight*, Seattle, Wash., August 23, is, I believe, the most Bolshevistic preachment I have seen in any colored weekly.

"UNCLE SAM ANGERS COLORED FOLKS

The colored folks of these United States are awfully angry with Uncle Sam. Their reason is logical, they have showed that they have had implicit confidence in his word, and followed every lead that he has prepared, bought thrift stamps, liberty bonds, went over the top, protested, supplicated, petitioned, all has been in vain, they believed in the honor of the present government in making good its pledge of making the world a fit place in which to live, to them Uncle Sam has prevaricated, things are worse; now they are angry and are paying more attention to the propaganda that is being spread and listening to the soft soothing words of the Soviets, Bolsheviks, Reds, and Radicals, they have no faith in the Democrats or Republicans, both have lied themselves out of the good graces of the thinking colored folks, and now what they want is some real positive, absolute actions against lynching and burning of their people, and are sure turning to the party that promises to better conditions, and offers them a ghost of a chance at least to protect themselves when the crisis comes. Any colored man with an ounce of sense knows that there is no assurance of the law protecting them from the atrocities of the mob, and knows that the lying press paints the picture with the colored man the aggressor, they also recognize the fact, that the government is too weak to discharge its obligations to law-abiding citizens, and is of no benefit to them, and any party for succor. It is human nature."

The colored papers' answer to the charge of Bolshevism is in the following editorials:

"False Alarm

We have just read a story in the New York *World* to the effect that the I. W. W., an industrial society, is inciting the Negroes throughout the country to rise up against the white folks. This society is composed entirely of white people. The story goes on to say, 'That congress is alarmed and will soon begin an investigation to verify the charges made against the race.' It is also indicated in the story that Congressman Ragsdale, of South Carolina, who died of heart failure while shaking hands with a physician, was killed by Negroes, and that Congressman Byrnes, another Negro hater from South Carolina, is threatened and that articles appearing in the *Crisis* and *Messenger*—two New York Negro magazines—are evidences that the Negroes are contemplating an uprising against the whites.

"Now, this story is too frivolous to believe and unworthy of a place in a great Metropolitan daily like the *World*. The *World*, as a rule, is a fair sheet—giving the truth on every issue and a square deal to every man, but the *Independent* is of the opinion that our contemporary is unduly alarmed. There are bad Negroes like bad white folk, and they sometimes give voice to radical and dangerous propaganda, but they in no more sense represent the bulk of the race than Emma Goldman, Berkman and Debs represent a majority of the white folk.

"There will never be an uprising in this country of blacks against the whites unless the whites precipitate it. The Negro can not always be expected to take what he has taken. He may be expected sometimes to strike back in self-defense, but he has no disposition to rise against the government in any section of our common country. He is law-abiding, peace-loving, conservative and patriotic, and the I. W. W., the Bolshevists and no other rabble of white propagandists can induce him to rise and undertake to exterminate the white man. In the first place, he knows he would get the worst of it—that the white man is best prepared to fight and that the government, both state and federal, would be used by the white man not only to suppress him, but to crush him. But he will not desist from uprising out of fear of a stronger arm but because of his love of law and order, his love of peace and his patriotism.

"We are glad to see congress move to make an investigation of the riots that are spreading over our country. But we regret that they are prompted only out of fear of bodily harm. They should be moved by a sense of patriotic duty, by their love of fair play and a square deal for every man.

"Congress and the white press are unduly alarmed. There is absolutely no cause for excitement because of the Negro. Congress ought to be moved to investigate the white man's rising against the Negroes. The Negro is not rising against the white, and if the *World* would inform itself before it writes its next story, it would see that there is a general uprising of lawlessness on the part of the white man against black folk throughout this country—not only for the crime of rape, but because of the white man's hatred for the black man.

"In Montgomery, Ala., just a few days ago three Negroes were lynched and one driven out of town because he raised his hat to a white lady he knew, and the same white men who participated in the mob in disposing of this useful Negro had been teaching the Negroes all their lives to raise their hats and respect white womanhood. In Upson County, Georgia, they have had a Negro in jail for more than three weeks charged with trespassing—cutting timber off of another's land adjoining his. The sheriff had to spirit the brother away to keep the mob from lynching him for cutting down a pine tree. At Gray, Ga., a few days ago, a mob lynched a Negro who was already sentenced to the penitentiary for shooting a white man. At Lincolnton, Ga., the *World* carries the new story, that two blacks were lynched by a white mob because they were charged with shooting a deputy sheriff. These Negroes were burned like brush in a new ground. A third Negro was shot and killed by the posse later, because he refused to give information which he didn't know, and many others were whipped and beaten senseless because they were unable to give information.

"With all these cold-blooded and dastardly murders going on all over the country by white men, there is no disposition on the part of the blacks where the crimes are committed to take the law in their hands—and the *Crisis, Messenger* and other radical Negro papers no more represent the thought, character and intelligence of the twelve million Negroes in this country than Emma Goldman, Debbs and other Bolshevists represent the conservative and intelligent class of our white neighbors.

"Congress is unduly alarmed."—*The Atlanta Independent,* October 11.

"Not Bolshevism—Just American Injustice

A report has gone out from Washington—and certain Southernized officials and Negro-haters are nursing it as a fact —that evidence has been discovered that Bolsheviki are at work among the Colored people of this country, and that 'the unrest and intense feeling' evidenced among the race are the results of our assimilation of the Bolshevist doctrines.

"These Southernized officials and enemies of the race are conventiently blind to the fact that the 'unrest and intense feeling' are caused by the following injustices which are heaped upon us:

"Denial of suffrage; hurtful and hateful segregation; jim-crow cars and other forms of discrimination; wholesale lynching of Colored men and women—women even about to become mothers.

"The practice of these injustices, which has caused our unrest had been going on long before the Bolshevist movement raised its slimy head in Russia, and our unrest has been magnified into 'intense feeling' by the disappointment we recently experienced when this country 'broke faith' with us after our sacrifices on Flanders' fields.

"There is 'intense feeling' among us because we have come to realize that we have no rights which a white man is bound to respect, a condition which no self-respecting race can tolerate with equanimity.

"We have not become tainted with the iconoclasm of the Bolsheviks. We do not plan to rebel against orderly government. But we want to remind the government that so long as it permits a group of its citizens to make a football out of law and order, so long will there be intense feeling and unrest among us.

"For officials of the national administration at Washington and the Negro-haters to nurse such a delusion as the report indicates, is to shut their eyes to the real fundamental cause for the 'unrest and intense feeling' among the Colored people in this country."—*The Cleveland Advocate,* October 18.

The trend of the counsel offered by the highest dignitaries of the colored churches will be indicated in the following utterance, widely printed:

"Knoxville, Tenn., Sept. 9.—Bishop George C. Clement of this city addressing a class at Morris Brown University said: 'I would urge all members of my race to obey the law and keep clear of Bolshevism and all incendiary suggestions. We must demand protection of life and property by the government, which is guaranteed as the surest antidote for Bolshevism. I believe my people should defend their homes and families. Certainly this crisis calls for great moderation and self-control. We still have faith in true democracy and expect a righteous race adjustment.' "

The attitude of the colored weeklies with not above three exceptions, if so many, is expressed, I believe, in the following editorial as concisely as may be. It is from *The Denver Star,* September 27:

"Negroes Steady and Pause

The Negroes of the U. S. must now, as never before, work, think, and reason to avert the threatening national chaotic crisis which looms behind strikes, discontent, mobs and burners of human flesh. The *Star* desires to emphasize the seriousness of these conditions which are spreading in one form or the other to every state. We are face to face with anarchy and bolshevism which is applied socialism gone to seed and which is more likely to directly or indirectly affect the happiness, peace, and prosperity and even the life of our people. An upheaval is slowly rising and Negroes must now think deeply, reason soundly and act slowly. Do not be swept aside too easily by disheartening and discouraging injustices to us and our race. We cannot win by and through hate, loss of the church or Christianity, exchanging what we now have for a condition far worse than what we now have. We are backed up to the wall and let each of our steps outward be a careful, systematic and progressive tread. Negroes steady, read with the idea of weighing and considering and not with the idea of accepting or rejecting. Steady, Negroes, and pause, for you may have to save America from herself yet. Be wise."

IX. NEGRO PROGRESS

1. *Miscellaneous Examples and Agencies for Uplift*

A VERY large proportion of space and prominence is given in colored papers to the progress of the race in the various fields of activity and departments of life. Articles and notes reporting and appraising racial achievements bear witness to that racial pride which the white man has so frequently commended to the colored man. I give here a disproportionately small space to this topic, but my design does not call for more.

A few items of news, widely printed, will serve as examples. "COLORED MAN WINS PREMIUM FOR FIRST BALE OF COTTON." This item tells how a Texas colored man after picking a bale of cotton hauled it by night to market and won a $25 prize. "He is the type of Negro," comments *The Phoenix Tribune*, "that is a credit to his race."

"EDITOR WINS PRIZE."

The editor of *The Phoenix Tribune* in a free-for-all statewide contest for proposing the best method of advertising a local automobile firm won first prize.

Many similar items are featured on the front page of colored papers.

"Southern Negroes Benefited by Clubs

Washington, Sept. 9.—Clubs organized among Negroes in the South by the department of agriculture and the state colleges are resulting in cleaner premises, wells and spring houses and better repaired houses and cabins, a review of the work, issued to-day by the department, declared. The Negroes embrace with eagerness the opportunity offered through the clubs to improve conditions of their homes, it was stated. In 1918, 1,563 rural Negro women's clubs were organized with

37,913 members and 1,962 girls' clubs were organized with a membership of 50,995. The total Negro club membership is 103,377.

"The Negro club women have organized 117 coöperative poultry breeding associations and fifty coöperative egg circles are the means by which they obtain a better price for their products."—*The Call* (Kansas City, Co.), September 20.

Articles of similar character are at hand on Farm Demonstration Work, Rural Improvement, etc. According to estimate there are a million Negro farmers in the United States and a quarter of them own the farms they occupy.

The two following items taken together unhappily bring back the direful situation:

"A Model Negro Town

A town which is wholly populated and conducted by Negroes, Hobson City, Ala., was started in 1900 by a band of Negroes who obtained a charter and incorporated the town. The population shows a gain of 150 per cent. No man without employment is allowed to stay in the town. Either a job is found for him or he is required to move away. The town has four churches, with a combined membership of 700, a good public school with 250 pupils, a dozen progressive stores, waterworks, electric lights, police and sanitary departments, a well-built jail, and a governing board elected every two years, consisting of seven councilmen, a mayor, and four other municipal officers, including a chief of police. It is the only town in the state that is out of debt and has money in the treasury. More than half the citizens own their homes."—*The Southern Workman* (Hampton, Va.).

"We see that a black hand letter surmounted by a skull and cross bones, usually used to spell death in all of its horrors, followed by an alleged assault against his person, by two unknown men is given as the reason for the departure for the North of Newman O'Neal, mayor of Hobson City, the exclusive Negro town near Anniston, Ala. A few weeks ago, the Hobson City mayor is said to have received a warning that he would be killed unless he left these parts immediately. A short time after the receipt of the letter, the mayor claimed that he had

been assaulted near his home, and announced to his friends
that he intended to obey the warning in the letter. Accordingly, he gave up his position as head of the government at
Hosbon City, and went north. Since his departure from this
section no other of the officers of the town have been recip-
ients of warning or black hand letters."—*The Charleston Messenger*, August 9.

The Negro Year Book, 1918-1919, gives sixty-four towns and
twenty-one settlements populated and governed entirely or
almost entirely by Negroes.

The Afro-American has a special aptitude for organization.
Friends of that race will interpret the trait as eminently useful, if wisely directed. Otherwise, it is pregnant with possibilities of disaster. The Negro's many organizations in all
the departments of his life were never before so prosperous,
or so active for good. From the Associated Negro Press,
January 1, 1920, I take the following summary:

"Agencies for Uplift

The national agencies for uplift among the Colored people
of the United States have increased in financial strength and
influence more than ever before. Among the strongest of these
agencies are the following:
Churches
Lodges
Schools
The National Urban League
The National Negro Business League
The National Association for the Advancement of Colored
People
Young Men's Christian Association
Young Women's Christian Association
War Community Work
National Equal Rights League
The Associated Negro Press
The National Negro Press Association
The Lincoln League
"These organizations cover every phase of the problems
of the entire group and their work is carried on with com-

mendable efficiency and even increasing support of the people
at large. The work of these various organizations attracts
not only the people of the group, but for 1919 especially the
leading forces among the whites have given serious consideration to their progress, and helpful coöperation of a
substantial nature. The results have been a more intelligent
understanding, and more wide-spread interest in the problems
of adjustment."

Constructive programs are put forth by the various Negro
organizations and appeals for coöperation in making them
effective are issued in their journals. The following is typical:

"Racial Coöperation

Hampton, Va.—The Negro Organization Society of Virginia (Allen Washington, Hampton, President), and the Negro
Teachers' Association of Virginia (D. G. Jacox, Norfolk,
President), speaking through a joint committee, of which
John M. Gandy, president of the Petersburg Normal School
and executive secretary of the Negro Organization Society,
is the general chairman, recently adopted the following educational and civic program.

VIRGINIA PROGRAM

"1. Growth and prosperity depend upon the habit and
spirit of coöperation. 2. Racial strength should be massed
for the advancement of the kingdom of righteousness and not
for the abetting of the kingdom of darkness. 3. The best
service can be rendered by workmen of intelligence and training. 4. Teachers must be adequate in numbers and efficient
through preparation and experience. 5. School terms should
be longer; school buildings should be well ventilated, well
heated, well equipped, and sanitary. 6. The education of the
young is the most vital concern of any people.

"7. Children should be sent to school every day the school is
in session. 8. Educational campaigns should be waged through
the public press, the pulpit, and mass meetings. 9. Everybody
should work in harmony and coöperation with the public-
school officials. 10. Everybody should be taught the value of
systematic saving. 11. The success of a race depends upon its

Negro Progress 161

ability to organize and develop business enterprises. 12. People should be encouraged to improve their farms and buy land. "13. Colored people in Virginia do not want social equality. 14. Public carriers should furnish equal accommodations for equal fares. 15. In city and country there should be a just distribution of advantages in living quarters. 16. There should be equality of wages for equal service rendered. 17. Public-school funds should be distributed equitably. 18. Opportunities should be provided for the secondary and collegiate training of colored youth."—*The Charleston Messenger,* October.

Special departments of organized activity will be treated in the following separate sections.

Among the agencies that represent practical coöperation the National Urban League is active in many and various departments of life. Its purposes and activities will be indicated in the following brief note:

"Working for a 'Square Deal'

The annual Conference of the National Urban League held in Detroit, Michigan, October 15-19, declares the Negro constitutes one-seventh of the American labor supply. And that he must be considered in any effort to stabilize the present condition of labor unrest. In speaking of the migration of the Negro northward and the South trying to lure him back, the league agrees to coöperate with any North or South that will give satisfaction and tangible assurance on the following:

"(1) That working and living conditions of Negroes will be fair and decent.

"(2) That transportation accommodations for Negroes will be equal to those provided for white people.

"(3) That adequate educational facilities will be provided for Negroes.

"(4) That the Negro will be given fair treatment, and be protected in buying and selling.

"(5) That the life and property of every Negro will be protected against all lawless assaults.

"(6) That the Negro will be assured of equal justice in the courts."—*The Foundation* (South Atlanta, Ga.).

2. Business

The general reaction of the Negro to the stress and strain of the present crisis exhibits many aspects. One of the most noteworthy may be covered by the word *business*. Into the business life of the nation he proposes to enter, and is entering, according to his papers, with a new purpose, energy, and unity. "Race patronage for race business" is the slogan here. In labor, in the trades, in commerce, in the professions, in all the material interests of life, segregation and discrimination and violence are bringing about this result—racial solidarity, racial coöperation. News items, editorials, and advertisements bear abundant witness to a new era in business for the Negro.

The discriminations of white insurance companies against colored people caused the withdrawal of thousands of policies, according to colored papers. In Jacksonville, Florida, according to *The Raleigh Independent*, 16,000 Negroes withdrew from an insurance company because two of its agents had participated in a lynching. There has been a great impetus thus given to colored insurance companies and large new companies are being organized.

The Dallas Express, November 22—to go once more beyond my time limit—has on its front page an article under these headlines, printed large:

"Negroes Launch Greatest Commercial Venture of Age. Mammoth Corporation for Development of Insurance Among Negroes Chartered by Negro Capitalists."

The Louisville News, October 18, contained the two following articles, which may well be thought of together:

"Arkansas Raises $100,000.00 for Race Business

Hot Springs, Ark., Oct. 16.—(A. N. P.)—The Overalls Manufacturing and Industrial Association, with an authorized capital of $100,000, has been organized and is meeting with success. The prospectus states that it has the purpose of 'operating a manufacturing plant, overall plant, furniture plant and other industries, giving employment to hundreds of men and women; to emphasize industrial features, to secure enough loan to develop manufacturing centers among our people, thereby opening the door of hope along industrial lines.' "

"Please Open a Ladies' Store

A woman told us the other day our discussions on business interested her very much. So much so that she was inclined to invest some money in a store catering to women specially. She added that COLORED WOMEN COULD NOT TRY ON GLOVES, CORSETS, HATS AND SHOES IN CERTAIN STORES! Ye gods! Why then should anybody hesitate to open a store that would cater to Colored women?

"But the woman in question discouragingly replied: 'Oh, what's the use? Colored women would go to these white stores just the same.' Can it be true? Can it be true that our women of intelligence and refinement and appearance would pass by a store of their own Race, catering particularly and especially to them and go buy, go spend their money in white stores that insult them? Surely not. Surely not. Surely not. And yet it is an insult to a Colored woman to tell her she cannot try on a glove or a hat or a corset or a shoe because of her color. But the Colored woman who buys under those conditions not only insults herself, but she insults US and she insults YOU.

Won't somebody please open a store, a first-class store, catering particularly and especially to Colored women, so that they may at least spend their money free from insult? Please."

The Savannah Tribune September 27, gave the following explanation of the new spirit manifesting itself in the Negro business world:

"While a great many things, including riots and agitation, labor and housing discrimination, are now stimulating racial self-consciousness, clannishness and fellow-interest among our people everywhere, it is well to launch these enterprises, North and South, organizing the people in economy and industry, conserving the strength by handling the financial turn-over, and as a result we shall be able to present a formidable organization and strength and skill for many of the other necessary and vital purposes.

"In the South, we are already at it to a marked extent; we are increasing our business activities every day, in almost every town. In the centers of Negro population in the big cities of the North, our people are arousing to the tremendous possibility presented them to handle the thousands of dollars which Negro wage-earners spend daily, weekly, monthly in the general processes of living. The food item, the clothes item, the amusement item, the rent item, all afford magnificent possibilities for Negro business genius. Most of the business should pass through Negro business channels, and it can be made to.

"Long as we have been coming to it, there are a great many ways by which one Negro can reach another which are closed or unknown to any white man. We are coming to possess and to betray many of the subtle elements of clannishness and espirit de corps which other peoples possess, and lacking which in the past, we have been the subject for exploitation by other peoples. Alas, we are discovering ourselves; we are being in a measure, driven to it; and it is going to inure to the marked benefit of Negro business organization and genius.

"It will make fortunes; it will make gigantic enterprises; it will create colossal institutions; it will create power."

The colored press generally contained an extended account of the 20th annual session of The National Business League held in St. Louis, August 13, 14, and 15. Editorials evaluating and commending its proceedings were numerous. This league was founded by Dr. Booker Washington, and its purposes and activities seem to be in accord with his principles. This session was attended by more than 1,000 out-of-town delegates. Addresses were delivered by successful business men. Dr. Robert R. Moton, principal of Tuskegee, was elected president, and Dr. Emmett J. Scott, for twenty years secretary to Dr. Washington and now secretary-treasurer of Howard University, was reëlected secretary. Dr. Scott's progressive reconstructive

Negro Progress

program was adopted, and it is now in process of being carried out, with headquarters at Washington.

To every phase and sphere of race enterprise the same spirit is extended. New banks, departmental stores, factories, insurance companies, business leagues, large land purchases, coöperative enterprises—such things are announced every week in all the colored press.

3. *Art and Literature*

Articles on the Negro's progress in the various fine arts—music, painting, poetry, dramatics—constitute a portion of the contents of most Negro papers. Elaborate articles reviewing the history of the Afro-American in this or that field of intellectual and artistic endeavor appear in the abler papers. It is in these articles that racial pride is most manifest. From *The Journal and Guide* (Norfolk, Va.), October 4, I have a column article under the heading:

"RAPID DEVELOPMENT OF THEATRICAL ART AMONG AFRO-AMERICANS

Refined Drama, Teaching Lessons of History, Cultivating Higher Ideals and Race Consciousness Taking Place of Cheap Vaudeville and Minstrelsy"

The erection and purchase of theater buildings and the establishment of a theater circuit in the larger cities of the country have been reported. By appreciative notices of dramatic productions, Negro authors are encouraged by the press to produce better and better plays. Articles such as the following are appearing in the colored magazines. It is taken from the *Praiseworthy Muse* (Norfolk, Va.), a newly established monthly, devoted, as its title indicates, to poetry, drama, criticism, and the arts generally. I quote but the last half of the article:

"The Negro and the Stage

By George C. Anderson, *The Wayfarer*

The Negro has made good in nearly every line of endeavor and has been accorded a fair recognition in nearly all of them, in arts, sciences, industries, music; but on the stage he has made a very poor showing and has been shown in a very unfavorable light. The reflection cast by the Negro from the great mirror of the stage is unfavorable to the ninth degree; it is not only unfavorable, it is degrading.

"The only class of Negroes which most people of other races are familiar with are of the 'monkey type,' and they are familiar with these because they are constantly before them in minstrels, as servants in shows, in pictures and even in some of the dramas. And worst of it all these characters purporting to represent colored people are not played by Negroes but by white actors who act their parts according to their personal conception of what the Negro really is. At their hands the Negro gets a mighty poor deal.

"While the white actors are largely responsible for this distorted conception of the Race, our colored actors are partly to blame. Nearly every colored actor blacks his face and tries to act the part of the southern ignorant Negro. If he plays 'straight,' he almost invariably plays the part of a white man using the Negro for the 'goat.' Too large a majority of the colored women on the stage to-day, while they do not black up as a rule, cast a black and distastful reflection by reason of the fact that their acts and the parts they play tend to represent the colored women as highly immoral creatures. Their songs nearly always represent 'my loving man' type and the lines they attempt have as their general subject 'my man.' This persistency of the colored actors to stick to the burlesquing of the Negro before the public is doing almost as much to keep down high ideals among the rising generations as the most radical Negro-hating white journal.

"What is needed is more attention of colored writers towards plays with Negro characters as heroes and the attention of colored actors to plays with Negroes as heroes instead of Negroes as clowns, servants, and petty criminals. In other words our mirror needs cleaning so that it will reflect a true image of Negro life instead of the distorted monstrosity which is shown us every time we see a play using a character representing the Negro."—*Praiseworthy Muse,* September.

In music the Negro exhibits unique and extraordinary genius. Encouragement is being given by the race to creative artistic work. The subject occupies a noteworthy proportion of space in the colored papers. The following announcement is significant:

"First Issue of Musical Monthly

Philadelphia, Pa., Oct. 27.—The *Master Musician,* a musical monthly for masters, artists, teachers, scholars and music lovers has made its initial appearance. The periodical is a twenty-four page magazine with cover and is replete with everything of interest to musicians. It is edited in a high class way and George W. Parvis is editor. The offices are located at 501 S. 16th street."

An art event of national importance in the Negro world occurred in St. Louis during the summer. An account with appraising comments appeared throughout the colored press. I take the following from *The Southwestern Christian Advocate* (New Orleans):

"Mural Tripartite Unveiled in Poro Building, St. Louis

The Negro loves art. Some day his vivid imagination will have full sweep and Negro artists will make the world their debtors. The Poro Company, St. Louis, has just given us a fore-taste of what the Negro will do when he has refinement that comes from intelligence and growth in the finer arts and when he has wealth with which to express his refinement. The Poro Mural has more than local significance. It is prophetic of the race.

"The mural Tripartite is in three panels: The first, Genesis; the second, Exodus; the third, Apotheosis. In the Genesis, the Negro is seen bearing a burden. The burden contains his entire earthly possessions, for he has but little, being a child of the desert. This represents the race's beginning or Genesis.

"In the Exodus, the Negro still bears his burden, but it is no longer a selfish one. It now consists of the fruit of his toil, the product of agriculture. There has also come into his life, a knowledge of the mechanical arts of which the presence of the hammer and cogwheel bear silent witness. The Apotheosis, the middle and largest panel shows what has been done through constant application and sacrifice. Three heroic figures of beautiful Negro womanhood personify Liberty, Music and Art. The presence of the Lyre on the side of Fine Arts and of Books on the side of Liberal Arts shows that in Literature and Music the race has made its most wonderful progress."

Critical essays and book reviews indicate a literary activity in the race which finds other channels of publicity than the newspaper. The modern note is sounded in all these articles. Many young writers are busy with their pens in the departments of history, biography, fiction, and poetry. I must, however, forego giving the evidence in quoted utterances.

4. Colored Womanhood

An exceptionally large space is given in colored papers to the work for and by colored women. Appreciation of womanhood and the influence of womankind is strongly in evidence. Protective societies and industrial and rescue homes for girls are reported as being established and supported. The following items are typical:

"Wilmington, Del., Sept. 11.—The State Federation of Colored Women of Delaware has at last succeeded in purchasing a site for the proposed Industrial Home for Colored Girls. Negotiations have been made and plans are now under way for the starting of the work in a short while."—*Associated Negro Press.*

"Home for Colored Children

A committee composed of different social agencies in the city, including members of the Civic and Commerce Association, met with Mrs. Maxwell to discuss ways and means to establish a home and day nursery for colored children. The committee will have more to say in the near future."—*The National Advocate* (Minneapolis), October 25.

"Permanent Community Center for Girls

A permanent Community Center for Girls is the slogan of the women of Portsmouth.

"A membership campaign is to be conducted by the committee on women and girls. All women are invited to join with this effort of the committee.

"The new worker in the person of Miss Fletcher Howell, will be here in a few days and it is hoped that she will unfold the policy of the W. C. C. S. in working with girls. All women are requested to visit the center in the next few days.

"You will find there a rest room where strangers waiting for boats or trains may rest for the day, you will also find a kitchenette which may be used. There is a gymnasium fitted up for recreation.

"It is earnestly hoped that the women of Portsmouth may make ample provision to keep such a place."—*The Journal and Guide* (Norfolk, Va.), October 4.

"In the interest of the young women of her race, Mrs. W. D. C. Carter of Seattle, Wash., general secretary for the Y. W. C. A. of that state, spoke. She said: 'No race can rise above its women, and if the Negro is to be lifted up he must turn attention to saving the women We should be interested in our women of the South who are forced to ride in dirty cars, who must pay first class fares and get third class accommodations, who are insulted by all classes of men. I want the young Negro girls saved, because upon them rests the future of the race.' "—*The Denver Star*, October 11.

From *The Advocate* (Portland, Oregon), I take the following news item which will indicate the organized efforts now being put forth by the colored women of America in politics and social uplift:

"The President of the National Association of Colored Women Issues Call to Colored Women of America to Join in the Great Fight for Human Rights

.   .   .   .

"Within a few days an appeal will be sent forth to Christian men and women throughout America to join the Woman's

Convention Auxiliary of the National Baptist Convention in ten days of prayer, including a day of fasting and prayer, November 25, and closing with a nation-wide prayer meeting Sunday morning, November 30, at 6 o'clock. We are calling upon the people to pray:

"First: For the United States government to protect the rights of all its citizens at home and to put an end to mob violence, lynching and the burning of human beings alive.

"Second: That righteousness shall go forth as brightness and justice as a lamp that burneth.

"Third: For a white ministry that will heed the command, 'Lift thy voice like a trumpet and show my people their transgressions and the house of Jacob their sins.'

"Fourth: For a press that will mold healthy public sentiment in favor of absolute justice.

"Fifth: For the Negro race to live up to every requirement of an American citizen.

"We call upon every woman in the National Association to bring this matter before the clubs and to coöperate heartily in carrying out the program that will be sent out by the women who inaugurate the movement. Let us pray; let us believe; let us work!

"At the present time the women in the states where the ballot has been given should be lined up and enlightened on the question of suffrage."

5. *Schools*

School opening in September called forth editorials very generally on the importance of education, with comments on inadequate facilities, overcrowded school-rooms, poorly paid teachers, and the inequitable division of taxes between white and colored schools. The following article from *The Southern Workman* (Hampton, Va.), was widely printed:

"The South and Negro Education

The Bureau of Education of the Department of the Interior published Bulletin No. 38 in 1916 relating to Negro education. The report showed that . . . the appropriations for teachers' salaries amounted to $10.32 for each white child enrolled, and $2.89 for each colored child, so that the appropriation per child was four times as great for each white child as for each Negro child. In some states the appropriation for each Negro child is less than one tenth the amount for each white child. The value of school property shows a similar discrepancy. In Alabama the Negroes constitute 41 per cent of the population and they have 10 per cent of the value of school property, and 11 per cent of the appropriation for salaries of public-school teachers. The average salary of white female teachers is $367 and of Negroes $172 per year.

"In South Carolina rural districts white schools are in session 130 days in the year and Negro schools 64 days. The average number of pupils per teacher in white schools is 23 and in Negro schools 46. The average teacher's salary is $395 per year for whites and $116 for Negroes; and the average expenditure for Negro pupils is about one-tenth as great as for whites."

The drift of the many editorials on the subject of schools and education is fairly represented by the following, from *The Birmingham Times Plain Dealer,* October 4:

"A Shortage of Schools

Ignorance begets crime, and until the masses of both races are educated, or given access to education, the intolerable conditions that exist to-day will be prevalent. And the demand that is here to-day for more schools should awaken us to the necessity of building more schools for our boys and girls all over the southland, as there never was a time in the history of our great country that the educated boy and girl were more in demand and each year brings on a greater demand for those who have gone to school and equipped themselves with that which is highly indispensable to their success in life (which is education). And the demand that is here for entrance into our various colleges should open our eyes to the indispensable need, which is more schools, that our boys and girls may be able to receive the proper literary training."

6. *Lodges*

The strength, activity, and importance of clubs, fraternities, leagues, lodges, and such organizations among the colored people will be indicated in the following articles. The call for the National Congress of Negro Fraternities, which was issued through the Associated Negro Press, contains important data. In part it was as follows:

"National Congress of Negro Fraternities

Springfield, Ill., June 29.—The National Congress of Negro Fraternities will hold its fourth Annual Session in Memphis, Tennessee, October 8-9-10, 1919. This promises to be the most important meeting in the history of the congress. Every district, state and national organization is urged to send its progressive, efficient officials or members to this meeting. Next to our church organizations, our fraternal societies are doing more to cement the Race, prove our worth as business men and women and raise the standard of our people along social and moral lines than any other agency. It is desired of the officers and members of this congress to make the fraternities a potent factor in the financial, social and industrial life of the Negro.

"We have over sixty fraternal organizations with a membership of over 2,000,000 men and women, whose combined wealth in cash and real estate represents over $100,000,000. The successful men and women of our Race are identified with some Fraternal Society. There is strength in union, and in this constructive age we must take advantage of every opportunity to give the world the best that there is in us. Let our slogan be, 'Take what you have and make what you want.' "

From *The Dallas Express* I take the following comment on secret fraternities:

"Among the agencies that count in the social, moral and civic uplift of the black people of the South and throughout the country, the secret fraternities may be counted as a source in which much good work is being accomplished. While nothing can ever take the place of the church and the school, the secret orders and the strong men and women at their heads, perhaps, come third in the advancement as a social center from which radiates that fellow feeling and racial helpfulness without which we should be at a loss for much mutual helpfulness in our forward trend."

The call for the National Congress of Fraternities would indicate that the lodges of all kinds are uniting their efforts, pooling their strength, working now with a common purpose and spirit. What is being done in particular cities and states will be indicated by this paragraph from *The Charleston Messenger,* August 30:

"The People's Federation

The People's Federation has been definitely organized and is now a part of our community. It seems destined to mean as much to the colored people of the city of Charleston as the League of Nations will mean to the people of the world. It is the most representative body that has ever been organized among our people in this city. Through it the religious, fraternal, business and social organizations can be united and can work together."

Notwithstanding the extraordinary number of lodges already in existence, and flourishing, still others are being founded for specific purposes, in response apparently to new conditions and needs. One of these was announced through the Associated Negro Press as follows:

"A New Thing

IN THE ENEMIES' LINES

The formation of the Lincoln League of America is a new departure. The white South wishes it thoroughly understood and advertised that in the matter of dealing with the Negro, its ideas shall prevail. Counsel, coöperation or advice have been consistently and persistently resented for the most part.

"On the particular subject of voting, the white South has openly and boastingly defied not only the Negro, but the United States government.

"Thus far, it has gotten away with both without any considerable trouble or worry. The strong possibility of Woman's Suffrage being attached to the constitution of the United States has recently caused considerable worry, and movements of the Lincoln League kind are calculated to cause trouble, in the event that logic and reason are eliminated in the program—and when it comes to dealing with the Negro, these two elements have never been pinnacled as it were."—*The Hutchinson Blade,* July 12.

The following resolutions were adopted by the sixteenth biennial session of the Knights of Pythias at Kansas City, August 30. They are representative of many such:

"And now, upon the return home of our Soldier Boys, with medals of honor upon their breasts, they are further denied everything that a human being should have—refused congenial labor and subject to race riots that are causing the United States of America to have to hide her face in shame; and reducing democracy to nothing but mere words.

"We utter this protest and demand that legislation more than mere words be formulated to correct present and prevent further outrages, and that a fair and equal chance be given us, as to the other people, in every walk of life."

It could hardly be expected that the colored man would lack the acumen to perceive the opportunity offered him in his lodge room to organize his efforts in his struggle for existence. In connection with this aspect of the topic *The People's Pilot* (Richmond), October, had the following editorial:

"Negro Fraternalism and the New Era

Negroes have never used the full strength of the LODGE ROOMS of secret organizations. When we were driven out of politics we took that energy into secret societies and the like.

"During the war, the Government appreciated the power that resided in the Negroes' LODGE ROOMS all over the country.

"We read that in many cases the doors of the secret societies were closed, fearing that the Negroes would foment dangerous things in their secret gatherings. In other words, it was feared that we had sense enough to use the power that resided in these orders.

"The day has come for us to use that power. In every Negro

'Society' at this time, there should be an hour set aside for real sensible constructive work. 'The Riding of the Billy-Goat,' Ritualistic ceremonies, hours of routine, of 'Roll Calls,' 'Working Nights,' the 'Grand' this and the 'Grand' the other—all those things might be set aside, modified, or simplified so that we may get the best results out of our splendid organizations all over the country. Instead of the 'old way' and 'old things,' we should have some leading man or woman to read a prepared paper on civics, education, the ballot, health, the State Government, the church, the suffrage, or some other outstanding momentous 'questions of the hour.' We should make these organizations our SCHOOL ROOMS during these trying times.

"Heretofore, when we wanted the 'Brotherhoods' and 'Orders' to help some charitable cause, we went before them and received their contributions. We see no reason why we may not go before them with '*Advice*,' 'Helps,' 'Suggestions, and teach our organized people how to fight, to the finish, the battles of LIBERTY and livelihood."

7. Churches

The Negro's interest in his church is one of his distinguishing traits. As between his lodge and his church it is not for the present writer to decide which has the greater importance and influence in his life. The two types of organization may not be in rivalry but coöperative. They both occupy much space in his papers. Schools, lodges, churches—they are a great trio in Negro life. To them add the newspapers. The important aspects of the Negro's religious life and of his church will appear in the editorials that follow. It will be observed that reference is constantly made to "these trying times."

"The Negro Church

The Christian Church is the greatest institution that exists among the colored people to-day. The Negro church represents a larger number of the members of the race than any other organization. It has the masses of our people in its membership, it has their confidence and they give it a support that is remarkable when we consider their small means. The churches have for a long time been the community centers for our people. The leaders of the church have very largely been the leaders of the community. It is also true that the church has molded the public sentiment of our race in a very large measure. They have been taught by the living voice of the man in the pulpit. He has been to them a source of information and inspiration. Through these critical times through which we are passing we trust that the Negro church may still have the leadership of the Negro race."—*The Charleston* [S. C.] *Messenger,* October 11.

"Dr. Hunter for Bishopric

There has been no period in the history of Afro-Americans when our great church organizations needed more than now the services of strong and capable men. These are perilous times, and unless signs fail there are critical times ahead, and we need as bishops, as preachers, and as leaders in every department of our racial activities the strongest men that we can summon to these places of leadership."—*The Journal and Guide* (Norfolk), October 11.

"The Minister as a Moral and Social Reformer

THIS IS THE DAY of opportunity for ministers of the United States, and especially for those identified with our group. With the stirrings of social unrest there are in spite of many handicaps ever widening fields opening to our men and women. The minister occupies the position of moral, spiritual and, in a sense, the social leadership of the Race. They have the ear of the people even more than a newspaper, for they reach a multitude of people who neither read nor think.

"WITH THE NEW CONSCIOUSNESS which has come to the Race in its desire for a fuller measure of civic and social justice, the voice of the pulpit should be most potential in inspiring and encouraging its efforts. But it should be equally as strong in pointing out the obstacles in progress which are created by our own people. It cannot be denied that we have a very large undesirable element in our citizenship everywhere—rough, uncouth and lawless. The church and the ministers should take them in hand."—*The Chicago Defender,* October 18.

It becomes increasingly evident to a reader of colored papers that the Negro is depending less and less upon white leadership in the church as elsewhere. The following editorial from *The Southwestern Christian Advocate* (New Orleans), October 23, bears witness to the strain and the alienation in process:

"THERE ARE OTHERS"

[Apropos of Dr. Mott's "Call on behalf of the young men and boys of the two great sister Anglo-Saxon nations."]

"We sympathize fully with the spirit of this Call. We recognize its urgency. We recognize also the increased pressure, strain and multiplied temptations and perils which the youth of the country face. The language of the Call is, however, exceedingly unfortunate and goes to prove how far wise men and good men may go astray in times of intense stress like these. Why a great body like the Young Men's Christian Association, that purposes to minister to all races, should plead exclusively for 'these millions of Anglo-Saxon youths' we cannot quite understand. For the Negro to claim that he was a part of the Anglo-Saxon youth would bring down wrath upon his head. There is no other interpretation of this Call than that the Negro youth is not included. Surely we do not forget how that 400,000 of Negro Americans, by their 'patriotic response to the call of country and civilization' and 'by their discipline and heroism' and 'by their devotion even unto death,' helped 'to establish the liberties of the world' and should have 'won the undying gratitude of their countrymen' of all creeds and of all races. Surely nothing in the history of America reveals so much that is worthy in the Negro and the 'comparatively latent capacities for adventure, for coöperation for sacrificial effort and for constructive achievement.' If the millions of Anglo-Saxon youths who were in the war face increased pressure and strain and multiplied temptations and perils, what shall we say of the increased strain and pressure and perils without limit that the Negro youth must face?

"Speaking of pressure and of strain, nothing but the grace of God holds the Negro steady at this time. And let us be thankful that the grace of God does hold him steady. The pressure and the strain through which the Negroes are now passing is something terrific. It calls for the strength of the superman and this strength is supplied by the presence of the

Divine Christ who counsels and advises and whose personal presence helps in these days of great stress and of peril.

"Surely we should pray for our Anglo-Saxon youth, but in God's name, there are many reasons more why we should pray for those Negro boys who are suffering more than the Anglo-Saxon youth suffer or will be called upon to suffer. Have we so soon forgotten our alliance and relation and duty to these men without whom and those of their kith and kin who came from the colonies of Africa, the achievement on the Western Front would not have been so glorious?

"Pray for the millions of Anglo-Saxon youth, of course. But there are others."

The following letter may be accepted as representing the sentiment of the entire colored people though it comes from but one denomination through its bishops. Other churches spoke to the same effect in conferences and conventions. These bishops are in the main Southern born and bred and now live in the South. Two at least were born of slave parents. They speak soberly the mind of the colored South:

"An Open Letter to the President and Congress of the United States and Governors of Several States

To the President and Congress of the United States and the Governors of the several States; as Bishops of the African Methodist Episcopal Zion Church, we feel called upon to address you upon certain serious conditions which do now obtain in our beloved country.

"We note with conscious pride the patriotic sacrifice which all the people of our own country made to secure the victorious peace in the great world war and to assure freedom for all mankind. With equal pride and hopefulness we trusted that this same spirit of patriotism and unanimity of action would continue throughout the period of reconstruction at least.

"We are both surprised and pained at the evidences of lawlessness and injustice so recently visited upon our people in various sections of our country. The lynching of Colored soldiers in American uniform, at Hickman, Kentucky, Hattiesburg, Mississippi, and other places, the savage mobbing of women and old men and the wholesale lawless and brutal attacks upon negroes even in the Capital of the nation, Longview, Texas, and the 'great city' upon the Lakes, cannot be overlooked by us nor by any others interested in the welfare of the nation and the perpetuity of our government.

"As the moral and religious leaders of a great denomination and the accredited spokesmen for hundreds of thousands of self-respecting and law-abiding citizens we ask the exercise of your good offices to correct these wrongs and prevent the recurrence of such outrages. We are not unmindful of the faults and shortcomings of some of our own race and we recognize that there are those who have not been altogether guiltless and being anxious that the American Negro prove worthy of citizenship in every respect, we pledge ourselves and all the agencies at our command to eradicate the evils among us and to promote harmonious racial relations and good citizenship.

"We believe that the demand of the American Negro for full civic and political rights is warranted by his services in times of peace and war. Among these rights which he would have guaranteed by the nation and the sovereign states are, the right to vote and hold office under the statutes without racial restrictions, the right to own and occupy real property wherever necessity may require and his means will allow, the right to work unmolested anywhere and at any time, at the accustomed wage accorded any other American citizen, the right of trial in a court of justice for any alleged offense, and the right not to be discriminated against on account of race in public places and upon all public carriers.

"We deem it wise to say in this connection that the question of social intercourse between the races has nothing whatever to do with the rights and privileges referred to above. Social fellowship between races, like that between individuals, is a matter of personal choice and is not to be confused with the indisputable rights of American citizenship.

"In respect to the un-American teachings of Bolshevists and anarchists we counsel our people to steer clear of them, thus maintaining their enviable record of patriotism and loyalty to our country. We feel that we voice the sentiment of the thoughtful members of our race when we say we cannot longer submit without organized protest to the injustices practiced against us in various sections of our country and we hereby appeal to the Christian spirit and principle of all the American people to make the highest and best contribution to the securing of the noble ends of justice for all the people.

"With the best wishes for the prosperity of our common country and for the maintenance of peace and good will between men, we are most respectfully Bishops African Methodist Episcopal Zion Church:

> Geo. W. Clinton,
> J. W. Alstork,
> J. S. Caldwell,
> G. L. Blackwell,
> A. J. Warner,
> L. W. Kyles,
> R. B. Bruce,
> W. L. Lee,
> G. C. Clement."

—*The Christian Index* (Jackson, Tenn.), September 11.

The rejection of white leadership and the alienation of the colored people from their own churches, with a loss of faith in Christianity, are results, according to the editorial spokesmen of the race, of these "times that try men's souls." The situation presents alarming aspects. There are omens of cults that shall be peculiarly the Negro's own. His aptitude for religion must be reckoned with. To illustrate this, partially at least, consider some of his readings of the evidences of retribution in the world's events and in nature:

"The King is Coming

"The King of Belgium is coming to Boston. While he is here every Colored American ought to wear mourning, to remind his Majesty of the treatment of our brother in the Congo. It should be recalled that the cruelty of Belgium excelled all other and remained so until an awful God turned peace into confusion and the bloody Germany mustered her great army and moved toward Belgium in what is known as the 'Teutonic drive,' August, 1914.

"King Albert and his cruel subjects fell victims to Germany and remained so until the American Black men stayed the hand and broke Germany's Military arm at Champaigne, Argonne forest. The King ought to know better than any one else the words of the Prophet, 'Vengeance is mine and I will repay.' "—*The Guardian* (Boston).

"God is upon the side of the Negro and will help him to prevail": that is almost the sum of the Negro's faith in the present year. In Texas no less than in Belgium he sees the law of retribution bringing disaster. One paper thus expresses it:

"It used to be said, and with a large percentage of truth in it, that every time the mob breaks loose and does inhuman cruelty to a Negro, Providence visits that section with some calamity such as cyclones or floods. Therefore, it comes right in line with this reasoning that Texas should tremble at the wrath of God, shown in an awful storm, when it has just finished the most dastardly crime that could be committed against us. We refer to the beating of Mr. Shillady of the National Association for the Advancement of Colored People. Texas has said by that act, that it not only does not deal fairly with its black citizens, but denies to even white men the right of free speech in discussing the condition of the blacks."

Another calamity in Texas is thus interpreted by *The Journal and Guide* (Norfolk), October 4:

"The Wicked Governor of Texas and the Hurricane

. . . .

Of course we sympathize with the stricken people of Corpus Christi in their misfortunes, and hope that they may be assisted to their feet again, but they should understand that one and one make two, and that when the whole state endorses mob lawlessness and justifies it by the words of their Governor, they have to pay for it, and pay for it dearly. The notion that a person or collection of persons, or a state or a collection of states can create an obligation without being made to meet the conditions of it at some stage of its maturity is not wisdom at all but unwisdom of the rankest kind.

. . . .

"Now, then, right on the heels of the dirty business [of assaulting Mr. Shillady], a hurricane and tidal wave visited

Corpus Christi, in Texas, and its surroundings, and killed some 300 people, leaving some 5,000 destitute and destroying some $10,000,000 of property values."

And in yet another Texas calamity retribution was seen. *The Freeman* (Indianapolis), October 18, presented the case under these headlines:

"TRAIN REFUSES COLORED PAS-SENGERS

Train Doing Rescue Work at Galveston, Texas, During Recent Storms and Flood Refuses to Permit Colored People to Ride on First one, it was Summarily Swept into Bay"

X. THE LYRIC CRY

Prayer of the Race That God Made Black

By Lucian B. Watkins

We would be peaceful, Father,—but, when we must,
Help us to thunder hard the blow that's just!

We would be prayerful: Lord, when we have prayed
Let us arise courageous—unafraid!

We would be manly—proving well our worth,
Then would not cringe to any god on earth!

We would be loving and forgiving, thus
To love our neighbor as Thou lovest us!

We would be faithful, loyal to the Right,—
Ne'er doubting that the Day will follow Night!

We would be all that Thou hast meant for man,
Up through the ages, since the world began!—

God! save us in Thy Heaven, where all is well!—
We come slow-struggling up the Hills of Hell!
                              AMEN! AMEN!

—*The Guardian* (Boston), August 30.

THE QUESTION

By Georgia D. Johnson

Shall I say, "My son, you are branded in this country's pagean-
    try,
Foully tethered, bound forever, and no forum makes you free?"
Shall I mark the young light fading through your soul-enchan-
    neled eye,
As the dusky pall of shadows screen the highway of your sky?

183

Or shall I with love prophetic bid you dauntlessly arise,
Spurn the handicap that binds you, taking what the world
    denies?
Bid you storm the sullen fortress built by prejudice and wrong,
With a faith that shall not falter in your heart and on your
    tongue!
                    —*The Crisis* (New York), August.

The Negro

Think ye I am not fiend and savage too?
    Think ye I could not arm me with a gun
    And shoot down ten of you for every one
Of my black brothers murdered, burnt by you?
Be not deceived, for every deed ye do
    I could match—outmatch: am I not Afric's son,
    Black of that black land where black deeds are done?

But the Almighty from the darkness drew
    My soul and said: "Even thou shalt be a light
Awhile to burn on the benighted earth;
    Thy dusky face I set among the white
For thee to prove thyself of highest worth;
    Before the world is swallowed up in night,
To show thy little lamp; go forth, go forth!"
                    —*The People's Pilot* (Richmond), October.

A Slave

My GOD! Tell me, just now, am I asleep,
Clasped hard by dull hypnotic Dolrum wave,
Am I a freeman, free to have, to hold,
Or am I still a cursed knee-bending slave?

They lynch me. Ah, they cut and burn my flesh,
And souvenir themselves with parts to save—
While I pass slowly on, unpitied, scorned.
A Slave! My God! A cursed knee-bending slave.
                    —*William Rufus Lackaye.*

Be a Man!

This must not be, the time is past,
When black men, laggard sons of Ham,
Shall tamely bow and weakly cringe,
In servile manner, full of shame.

Lift up your heads, be proud, be brave,
Though black, the same red blood flows through our veins,
As through your paler brothers;
And that same blood so freely spent on Flanders' field,
Shall yet redeem your race.

Be men, not cowards and demand your rights,
Your toil enriched their Southern land;
Your anguish has made sweet the sugar corn,
And drops of blood from the cruel master's whip
Have caused the white cotton to burst forth in mute protest.

Demand what is right,
Not a weak suppliant demand;
But an eye for an eye, and a soul for a soul,
Strike back, black man, strike!

—Carita Owens Collins.

Rise! Young Negro—Rise!

By John J. Fenner, Jr.

Ho! we from slumber wake!
Rise! young Negro—rise!
Begin our daily task anew—
Thank God we're spared to—
Rise! young Negro—rise!

Thy task may be an humble one.
Rise! young Negro—rise!
However great, however small,
Honesty and respect for all—
Rise! young Negro—rise!

Each has a race to run.
Rise! young Negro—rise!
Enter now while we're young,
Though weak and just begun.
Rise! young Negro—rise!

Our banner flown will some day read:
Rise! young Negro—rise!
Victory's ours! We've won the race!
Then let us live in God by grace.
Rise! young Negro—rise!
—*The Praiseworthy Muse* (Norfolk).

If We Must Die!

If we must die, let it not be like hogs
    Hunted and penned in an inglorious spot,
While round us bark the mad and hungry dogs,
    Making their mock at our accursed lot.
If we must die, let it not be like hogs
    So that our precious blood may not be shed
In vain; then even the monsters we defy
    Shall be constrained to honor us, though dead!

Oh, kinsman! We must meet the common foe;
    Though far outnumbered, let us still be brave,
And for their thousand blows deal one deathblow!
    What though before us lies the open grave?
Like men we'll face the murderous, cowardly pack,
    Pressed to the wall, dying, but—fighting back!
—*Claude McKay.*

The Octaroon

One drop of midnight in the dawn of life's pulsating stream
Marks her an alien from her kind, a shade amid its gleam.
Forevermore her step she bends, insular, strange, apart—
And none can read the riddle of her strangely warring heart.

The stormy current of her blood beats like a mighty sea
Against the man-wrought iron bars of her captivity.

The Lyric Cry 187

For refuge, succor, peace and rest, she seeks that humble fold
Whose every breath is kindliness, whose hearts are purest gold!
—*Georgia Douglas Johnson.*

Be Determined

Have you ever thought of doing
    Anything that is good at all,
Have obstructions blocked your pathway
    And at times you seemed to fall?
Listen, and let me advise you,
    Let me tell you what to do:
Hold up your head and keep a-going
    (And the goal will not be far).
Then to make the greatest showing
    Let the world know what you're doing.
Let the world know who you are!

Never stop for disappointments—
    Let nothing bar you from success.
Surely you will win the battle
    If you try your level best;
If you do as I advise you,
    If you do as I say do;
Hold up your head and keep a-going
    (Sure the goal will not be far)
Then to make the greatest showing
    Let the world know what you're doing,
Let the world know who you are!

When, at last you have accomplished
    The great aim you had in view,
Will you give some other brother
    The advice that I gave you?
Bid him do as I advised you—
    Tell him do what I said do:
Hold up your head and keep a-going
    (And the goal will not be far)
Then to make the greatest showing
    Let the world know what you're doing.
Let the world know who you are!
        —*Julia Davis Golden.*
In *The Bluff City News* (Memphis).

A Message to the Modern Pharaohs

("Loose him and let him go"—John 11:44)

"Loose him!"—this man on whom you plod—
Beneath your heel hate-iron-shod;
His silent sorrow troubles God—
            "Let him go!"

There will be plagues, wars will not cease,—
There cannot be a lasting peace
Until this being you release—
            "Let him go!"

Each doomful kingdom—throne and crown—
Built on the lowly fettered down,
Shall perish—lo, the heavens frown—
            "Let him go!"

Naught but a name is Liberty,
Naught but a name—Democracy,
Till love has made each mortal free—
            "Let him go!"

"Loose him!" He has his part to play
In Life's Great Drama, day by day,—
He has his mission, God's own way,—
            "Let him go!"

"Loose him!" 'Twill be your master rôle,
'Twill be your triumph and your goal:
'Twill be the saving of your soul—
            "Let him go!"
            —*Lucian B. Watkins in the Richmond Planet.*